TRAVELS

Hamish Brown

Travels

by HAMISH BROWN

THE SCOTSMAN
and
G.R.F. SUTHERLAND & Co.

Originally published in book form 1986

by The Scotsman, 20 North Bridge, Edinburgh
and
G.R.F. Sutherland & Co.

Typeset by Waverley Graphics Ltd., Edinburgh.
Printed by Ivanhoe Printing Co. Ltd., Musselburgh.

Contents

List of Illustrations

INTRODUCTION

W HEN I was asked to collect together the articles which had appeared over the years in *The Scotsman* and the *Evening News* I was panic-stricken in case there were too few to justify such treatment. In the end however only some of the material is being used. There are fewer foreign items because many "first accounts" of them were expanded into chapters of *The Great Walking Adventure* book which appeared this year. On the other hand I have included pieces which were first-mentions of trips which became books in themselves (chapters 3 and 4). Books as far as I'm concerned should lead to other books and I make no apologies for constantly recommending titles which have interested me on any particular place or topic. The pieces are arranged partly in chronological order and partly in thematic groupings and while each can be read at a random dipping there is also an element of continuity. A few linking notes have been added where I think this will help. I have not tried to re-write or change the articles so they still reflect the mood and style of their time, a range of twenty years. My thanks to all staff at *The Scotsman* who have helped make this collection possible. I would like to take this chance too, of thanking many readers for friendly (usually!) contacts and comments over the years. We have a splendid heritage, a rich tradition. May the next score of years deal kindly with it, and you, and this gangrel on his travels.

Hamish Brown
Taroudant, 1986

Also published by The Scotsman and G.R.F. Sutherland & Co.

The Morris File
by Albert Morris
(1985)

A humorous collection of favourite writings by Albert Morris of The Scotsman. Hugely successful in its first year.

"There is no-one like him for the sonorous rodomontade, the tin whistle blown like a trombone, the black board chalk squeak made mellifluous. Long may his quill quiver."—*Scottish Medicine*.

£3.95 nett

The Morris File—Volume 2
by Albert Morris
(1986)

By popular demand we publish this year another refreshing selection by Mr. Morris.

"I have the equivalent of thirty bob burning a hole in my pocket; Musselburgh looms sunnily on the journalistic horizon. While health, strength, inspirations and circumstances permit, I'll just carry on columning."—*A.M.*

£3.95 nett

Orkney Days
by Christine Muir
(1986)

Christine Muir's wonderfully descriptive writing conjures up vivid images of the flora and fauna, the happy life, the seasons, the sky, the sea, of this hard unyielding island, North Ronaldsay, at the most northerly tip of The Orkneys.

£3.95 nett

1. An Early World of Books

I do not remember learning to read. I do not particularly remember being read to either but, looking back, I simply see books as an integral part of existence.

They were always there; used and treasured. To this day I could describe the oatmeal-coloured textured cover of a book of Antarctic exploration, which is one of the earliest I can recall.

As I travelled from Ceylon to Scotland to Ireland to India to Japan to Malaya and, eventually, as a war refugee to South Africa, perhaps I have reasons for NOT remembering the learning process. It happened in so many places where people and events, sometimes terrible, fill the memory. My first clear remembrance of books dates to our years in South Africa.

Children are remarkably adaptable. In Malaya, I had been sent off to a convent school for safety and was soon crossing myself devoutly: I spent two years in South Africa and by the time I left had a nasal accent and spoke good enough Afrikaans to be top of the class. (I cannot remember a single word of it now).

I suspect Afrikaans included a great deal of history and story rather than the mechanics of language itself. South African history is exciting and romantic, heady reading for a juvenile bookworm. So I fought at Rorke's Drift and marched on the great trek over the Drakensberg. How superbly illustrated the books were in those days. Bulpin's were treasured and how unlucky the child who does not possess a copy of "Jock of the Bushvelt".

I had an aunt in South Africa and she smoked non-stop, making up for the rest of the family who do not smoke at all. Her cigarettes came in small round tins which were fascinating in themselves and, better still, contained cigaretts coupons. Two sets were on the go: "Our South African Birds/Ons Suid-Afrikaansa Voels" and "Our South African Flora/Ons Suid-Afrikaanse Plantegroei." For some small sum I acquired the two big books to go with them. The bird book I completed; the flower one had 11 blanks when we returned to Britain. My parents, rather meanly I felt, would not stay in Natal until I manged to obtain these, but I brought the treasured volumes home—and have been a life-long bird and flower enthusiast.

Over 30 years later in McNaughton's Bookshop on Leith Walk I

11

found several of these bird and flora books. None was complete, but I bought the lot for a pound and returned home with a gambler's fever. Could I gain 11 vital cards from this unlikely job lot? I did complete the book and, being a Fifer by descent and adoption, sold the rest again for the pound they had cost!

Dollar is about two miles out of Fife, a small village tucked under the friendly Ochils. A shepherd boy from those hills had gone to sea and made a fortune which he left to his home village and from this had come the famous school to which we boys were sent.

We were three brothers, born in Scotland, Ceylon and Japan, so were officially "foreigners" in school parlance.

Our private League of Nations was completed with mother born in Siam, and father, thankfully, born in Dunfermline. We all went through school playing cricket (tea with Learie Constantine), being bloodied at rugby (uniforms and caps round the Murrayfield area), divided for each sport into rival teams of "Britishers" and "Foreigners."

I was a shocking team games player and would much rather have been off alone on the Ochils, dog at heel and book in pocket, while athletics simply left me wondering how silly people could be. Studded cricket boots gave marvellous grip on the steep and slippery grass slopes of the Orchils. On one notorious Saturday I went off to the hills after breakfast, revelling in a golden spring morning and only, hours beyond recall, remembered I was supposed to be playing rugby that morning.

It was in English that I was most lucky. I would romp through the set work and then look about for mischief. The teacher, a quiet gentleman, was fair game, but he hit back. As soon as he saw me free, and before I could cause trouble, he would slip an open book on my desk with a quiet: "Read that."

My fondest Dollar memory is the family, deep in books, before a blaze of fire, while the radiogram played old seventy-eights of classical music. I am so glad I knew that world. You carried coals and sawed wood for the fire. It took six records to complete a symphony. But there seemed to be time for everything.

My appetite for books was no doubt adolescent, in quantity and quality, seldom related to the curriculum and has a great deal to answer for in later life. I am still a voracious reader, as unselective and as greedy. Life suddenly is all too short and time limited, so I am seldom without a book. The house is full of them. My motor caravan has a library and even on expeditions abroad or simply walking the home hills no camp site would be complete without its books.

The historian, novelist, architectural expert Nigel Tranter writes as he walks. I have not tried this, but I do tend to read and walk together, sometimes with unhappy results. I have fallen into several ditches, travelled miles past my destination and even walked into the wrong house. In East Africa during National Service we used to actually read aloud on long motor journeys.

I first met the books of C.S. Lewis while motoring across Uganda to the Mountains of the Moon. My work gave me long hours of quiet and parcels of books would come from long-suffering parents to satisfy the demands of those night watches.

National Service gave time to write as well, serving the lonely apprenticeship that twenty years on would actually see me called "author and traveller." It is strange how the things of childhood reach out to the future. Even before National Service days I would still have a book in the pocket. Paperbacks were invented at just the right time. Even as a boy roaming the Ochils I would often have a book with me. Most Kipling or Stevenson or Buchan I read lying on the broken slopes above Castle Gloom or the Burn of Sorrow.

All the influences and atmospheres combined to make the future certain, however unexpected. It was inevitable I would write as well as read, but not exclusively, for life is too rich to be narrowed down to one groove. In the Ochils I even ran into a real, living author who had a great influence on me in quite non-literary ways. It was odd that a school set below hills should have done nothing to encourage pupil interest in mountains and mountaineering. My parents were walkers and outdoor people, and so this freedom was naturally ours, but it was one largely pursued alone or with a few friends one infected.

W.K. Holmes, a minor poet and publisher's reader, was also fascinated by everything around Dollar, so we met regularly in the hills; he was the only adult we did meet, apart from shepherds. He would benignly watch us banging in six-inch nails as we pitoned our routes up the north face of the local quarry—we had been reading "The White Spider." Holmes' modest "Tramping Scottish Hills" became a treasure, annotated and quoted as we slowly discovered the hills he wrote about.

During and just after the war we went on family cycle tours, whole weeks spent in the Highlands before the tar went down on the Road to the Isles or "B and B" signs were invented. I am glad to have had that experience too, the sort of adventuring inimically described in Alistair Borthwick's "Always a Little Further". Later, we read W.H. Murray and became mountaineers, but as kids we just sucked it all in with the fresh air we breathed. When we could outpace our parents they sent us off alone. We were encouraged to go alone, to look after ourselves. This was my real education.

Truth is much more strange, complex and unbelievable than fiction. I would like to write more fiction, but find reality almost all-consuming of precious writing time. Writing at all has to be done in an unhappy combination with travel and mountaineering, a dual profession which leaves no time whatever for boredom, continuity or repetition, those ugly sisters of so many lives.

Much fiction, I suspect, is disguised reality, often even of personal connections. My teaching years were spent taking youngsters into the hills, pioneering in what has become the sterile fields of "Outdoor Education" with its "simulated adventure" and bureaucratic dead hand—which is why I left it. Bed-time stories were a regular feature, which the girls and boys (from the mining hamlets of Fife) found novel and interesting. Books are so often mystery objects simply from lack of acquaintance. In the wilds these kids looked up flowers in books, they read up climbs in books, they wrote their own log books and reported for a school paper. The mystery vanished. They began to read—for joy.

The mountain world has suffered a long spate of books by super stars about super climbs on remote and unpronounceable peaks, all deadly serious and often dully repetitive. My modest "Hamish's Mountain Walk," I think, has had such a warm reception simply because it is about our own, homely hills and all that lures us to them—anyone can associate with it.

That book was largely written in Morocco between active mountaineering ploys. I first went to Morocco because of an enthusiastic account by author Tom Weir and personal contact with Gavin Maxwell. Later, I was to read the latter's "Lords of the Atlas" and subsequently met some of its characters in Marrakech.

Thus, the bewildering mixture of fact and fiction, reading and writing, deep-seated Scottishness and world-wandering is not surprising. I have never been able to separate them.

Books have undoubtedly been vital in my life. Be warned then and think twice before you buy your youngster a book token for Christmas or slip a book into his pocket. You give him dangerous liberty.

For a decade and a bitty my classroom was the wilds of Scotland. It seems a long time ago now and not infrequently I am hailed (anywhere in the world) by men with less hair and greater girth who turn out to be old Braehead pupils. I wish, now, that I had written something more permanent about their activities at the time. The heading of this piece, written twenty years ago, halfway through my Braehead years, echoes the title of a book by our redoubtable headmaster, R.F. Mackenzie and re-reading it and dipping into his book I don't really think much has altered. Education, for generations, has been aiming at the wrong targets and firing with the wrong weapons. "A Question of Living" (1963), "Escape From The Classroom" (1965) and "The Sins of the Children" (1967) should be compulsory reading for all who have children at school.

2. Braehead: A Question of Living

FOR seven years I have had a unique teaching position at Braehead School in Fife. Though I came to this ordinary junior secondary school to teach English and Biology I was soon seconded, as it were, to "Expedition work"—camping and climbing throughout the Highlands and Islands. Out of this thousand and one nights and days with young teenagers has come probably an unrivalled knowledge of that age group's capabilities.

At week-ends now I am quite likely to be picked up by some former pupil and whisked off by his car to Glen Coe or Ben Nevis to be led up routes I could never lead myself. They have been to the Alps and further afield, the school club itself has grown up to become a member of the Association of Scottish Climbing Clubs. (Now the Mountaineering Council of Scotland.)

There had always been an interest in outdoor work (the school had a bothy by Loch Rannoch) but it was only when someone as uncluttered as myself could go at it full time that it became the main escape route for boys (and, to a lesser extent, girls) bursting with energies so poorly catered for in our Victorian educational set-up. Canoeing, gliding, boatbuilding, ski-ing, drama, art, music—

additional outlets multiplied. Simultaneously the crime rate fell, discipline was easy and school was a happy place.

It would be tempting to study the educational aspects but as the headmaster, R.F. Mackenzie, has written three books on the theories and practices of the school I just want to mention certain aspects of the mountaineering side of the work.

This began on local crags like the Maiden Rock at St Andrews, or week-end expeditions to the Arrochar or Crianlarich hills; everyone obviously enjoyed it. Then I was given a small gang of thugs to take to Glen Coe Youth Hostel. Their combined criminal record was extensive, their background appalling, their manners uncouth and their behaviour anti-social. Handed a packet of soup and told to put it in a pan, they did just that.

As I gazed at the unopened packet sending up an acrid, metallic smoke from the stove, I could hardly foresee that a few years later one of the culprits would have an account of his climb of the Grand Casse in the French Alps used in a text-book of prose passages; that he would sit at the same dinner table with members of the Alpine Club who had climbed on Everest, engaged in equal, animated conversation.

Yet I have been told—frequently (usually by those with "thirty years teaching experience")—that what I was doing was not education, but a waste of public monies, a grand "skive," of no lasting value. Deeds, fortunately, silence critics. Its educational value struck me every time I saw my best boys creamed off into "O" grade classes—where expedition opportunities were heavily curtailed.

That first expedition to Glen Coe was luckily blessed with fine winter conditions. We climbed every day: on the Buchaille, on Bidean, along the Aonach Eagach. Similar parties followed to Glen Coe again, to Glen Nevis, the Cairngorms, and a summer holiday wandering from An Teallach to Skye.

The years since have taken us to every area of Scotland. I began to regret my offer of a hotel "slap-up-meal" for those who passed their 50th "Munro" (which usually takes people a few years), when five occurred at once. (Later boys in fact left at 15 having passed the 100 up!) A look at rock-climbing or winter climbing records would show notes of new climbs ranging from Kilbreck to Sgriol, Skye, Rhum or Rannoch. And in the last "great year" stands the traverse of the Cuillin Ridge in Skye by three 14-year-olds, a day which is the dream of many adult climbers, a climax to mountaineering ambition.

Looking back, this growth has been a mirror of general climbing history. Attitudes and outlooks today have altered, and in our short history there has been the same rise in standard. In the early days an ascent of Curved Ridge impressed or defeated a small party; now the beginner will romp up and down it, or look critically at climbers on Rannoch Wall or the East Face of North Buttress—hoping to be there themselves before too long.

In the early days the boys, like the Victorian pioneers, faced all sorts of barriers—many of them psychological—which took time to break down. We were lucky that the first parties did enjoy it, and returned enthusiastically.

Many of them still climb. Then they were ill-clad (donkey jackets with shoulder patches burnt by abseil ropes were almost a badge), ill-equipped, doing something quite new in their own experiences and that of their home mining community.

They pioneered the "golden age" when everything was new and wonderful. One hundred Munros fell to the school in that first year; eventually, every 3000 ft. summit in the British Isles was to go. Bitter-sweet progression. There was something wonderful in that first careless rapture that echoed the tweeds and alpenstocks of the mid-nineteenth century.

On their heels came the "silver age": consolidation, filling in the gaps, widening summer and winter techniques, improving equipment, a swelling of numbers and a change in local outlook. It became respectable.

There were some fine days; a great winter traverse of Nevis, Carn Mor Dearg and the Aonachs demanding over 4000 ft. of step-cutting (no crampons in those days) or a summer romp from the C.I.C. Hut to Nevis summit in under a hundred minutes by Tower Ridge—a pupil leading.

We had our period equivalent to the sluggish inter-war doldrums. Yet the first new routes were done at this time. The World Wars in fact, were paralleled by my twice having leave of absence to lead over-winter expeditions to the High Atlas Mountains in Morocco. (1965, 1966.) The parallel was continued: the return from my second

Braehead days recalled—the 1967 team on Garbh-bheinn at the start of the Cuillin Ridge traverse (Bill Simpson, Tom Izatt, Hamish and Steve Menmuir)

absence, far from having set things back, brought a surge forward comparable to that following the war and Coronation Everest.

Three pupils and a former pupil achieved the complete traverse of the Mamores in eleven hours (fourteen is considered good time), while another party, one Easter in winter conditions in Glen Affric, produced a six days' tally of 45 peaks over 3000 ft., entailing 85 miles of travel and 32,000 ft. of ascent.

The first former pupil visited the Alps (and on the Meije, a difficult peak, survived an avalanche which continued to kill the next party; then faced the agonising descent, abseil after abseil, through a lashing storm).

Numbers grew again, yet skill increased: it was fun to report to the "old" 18-year-olds that the lads were now climbing a V.S. route without pitons where they, the first to climb it, had used two.

Today, international climbing knows no bounds; nothing is impossible—the winter traverse of the Cuillin Ridge, the Old Man of Hoy, the Matterhorn Norwand in winter, the Harlin Route on the Eiger. My dream was a schoolboy traverse of the Cuillin Ridge, which had twice before defeated us by weather.

In Skye it is usually too wet to climb or too hot to want to; yet, in a heatwave last summer, three 14-year-olds and I did this ridge: 10,000 feet of climbing which has taxed or defeated many competent parties.

It took nineteen hours of effort. At the end they were climbing with greater elan than ever, and far from being tired raced off the last peak to see who could be first into a bathing pool. I was fourth.

Their history has caught up on the wider history, their side stream joined now with the main stream, a tributary contribution to a fast flowing prospect.

Another interesting aspect has been what might be termed the psychology of these seven years. The two are closely connected, of course, but that they have done such things so young, so competently, above all so happily, has its reasons. These boys leave school at 15 or, if in "O" grade classes, at 16.

Only once in this period was there a pupil-made fiasco which involved other people; only once did a pupil break a bone (falling off a swing on a tree); yet the responsibility they were given and the risks we took were probably greater than usual among young people's

Braehead lads skating on Rannoch Moor with Blackmount Hills in background

mountaineering activity. This is not a boast (part of the cost of it is no doubt seen in my grey temples—the fatal accident may be tomorrow!); but the fact is worth assessment.

I have already briefly mentioned two big traverses: in both, 14/15-year-old leaders were responsible for making depots or joining in at stated times and places on the ridges, retrieving camps, preparing cooked foods and so on. In every case they did so effectively.

The Mamore party managed to make a geological collection along the ridges, enjoyed an impromptu swim and five minutes after reaching Glen Nevis Youth Hostel were being yelled at to stop playing "tig" round the dormitory. They were still children.

One of the support parties had a malingerer, and the boy in charge sent him back to the advance camp, saw him there, then raced his party up by compass into the snowy murk of Binnean Mor to have hot Bovril ready on time. That evening he was back with the advance base tents at Steall where we were staying, and had a meal ready for the other support party which returned over the Devil's Ridge and Sgurr a' Mhaim, having bagged a round of peaks. It was a complicated exercise ably carried out.

The Cuillin Ridge was an even bigger proposition, of course. Yet the same spirit prevailed. THEY demanded to add Sgurr na h'Uamha, which many illogically leave out and the descent was done at a trot.

Well acquainted now as I am to these lads' doings, I look back on this as one of the most incredible days of my life: that for nineteen hours fourteen-year-olds could steadily climb through that intolerable heat, where a single slip could have been disastrous, and end it, not desperately, but with verve and vigour to spare.

Only once have we had the miserable experience of picking up the telephone to launch a rescue: the culprit—a teacher who had joined our Hogmanay Meet.

I had taken a boy of fine winter climbing ability for a hard route up a peak while this teacher, a winter novice, went with two other well-experienced lads to skirt round the cliffs on easy ground and meet on top. To our horror, we saw this trio later shed a solitary figure who set off straight up the crazy face of the icy peak. Not for a minute did we consider it to be one of the two boys!

Sure enough they reached the cairn as we did; in appalling

conditions that drove us down after twenty bitter minutes with frostbite a real danger. An attempt to go up the face after the vanished teacher was defeated by wind and continual spindrift avalanches. Back at base we set about the rescue procedure.

The boys had everything they needed with them to deal with almost any emergency—except the situation that did arise. Who could have foreseen it? The teacher demanded "a short cut" up the cliffs! They quietly explained, correctly, both that the proposed route was impossible and that they were in the habit of keeping to instructions. On that they stood. What a moral situation to be faced by schoolboys!

The teacher, without map, compass or any experience of winter climbing, quite incredibly set off alone, followed mistake with mistake and probably owes his life to luck and an unusual sudden rise in temperature overnight.

On another meet to Glen Coe an Englishman asked if he could join us (myself and two experienced boys). As he recited a list of climbs done and sounded quite capable, I said this would be fine: he could go with one lad, I with the other, and we could make parallel routes up the North Buttress of the Buachaille.

We set off, and for twenty minutes were hidden from each other; then, on meeting, it was to find the pupil leading and from his stance gently "talking-up" a very frightened partner. I did not dare say anything until the thousand feet of ice-plastered rocks were below, and easy snow led to the summit.

The "experience" of this fellow simply did not contain any idea of big, verglas-covered routes; again we see a boy quietly making big decisions, and rising to fine leadership.

Both these incidents basically arose from the adults' self-deception: that they must, because adult, be wiser than "kids." The kids, of course, in their few years had gained an experience most average adults would gain only in a decade. From their concentrated experience, with its technical knowledge, its practice and procedure, had come the ability and confidence that could cope with situations like these.

In another severe storm in the Cairngorms we were battling on happily for Corrour off the blasted tops. Worry? Yes, for me; for the rest, confidence from known facts. A face all twisted by the wind pressed close to mine to yell:"Is it bad enough to dig in a snow-cave yet?"

Another, older boys' party, again from south of the Border, was hit by the same storm, one beyond any of their experience, so panic resulted and fatality followed.

I am sure that loss of confidence—mental despair—is a big contributory factor to "exposure," the physical collapse brought on by the actual conditions. Young people are probably tougher than we give them credit for, but mental toughness is something that has to be built up. It is hardly likely to be found in casual courses at centres, where they may be drawn from various school, industrial or youth organisations. They are droplets in a bucket being plunged into they know not what.

Our boys, year after year, are part of a gang engrained with a tradition. The bucket itself is permeated. Morale stays high because there is nothing to be afraid of; uncertainty is replaced by a happy trust, not blindly given but based on understanding. They themselves set, demand or follow a high standard. Indiscipline is regarded, rightly, as disgraceful; the boys themselves are the first to criticise any lapse.

Physically, too, these young teenagers still have a neatness, a co-ordination of mind, eye and limb which the older teenager often looses. The awkwardness of the adolescent is proverbial, and puberty brings not only physical but mental stresses and strains that produce uncertainty.

This is partly why so many Scottish accidents happen to non-Scots. Parties find themselves in overwhelming situations, lack of experience links hands with uncertainty, and the outcome is often disastrous.

We try to involve the pupils in every aspect of expedition work: working out food lists in school, planning routes, teaching each other, cooking and camping—the many facets of any expedition. Out of this comes an all-round, sane and balanced personality.

Which brings us to humour. If mountaineering is not fun, especially with youngsters, then it is a failure. Nor do I mean fun in the sense of that pleasure that comes when you stop banging your head against a stone wall.

Those nineteen gruelling hours on the Cuillin Ridge were made of magic minutes, each flying in pulsing enjoyment; there was always laughter breaking out from the larger, deeper content. On the most depressing days wind, rain or sun will soon cheer the party. The sheer challenge of the elements can set the soul singing: some of the hardest tussles are the most vividly recalled and most noisily discussed years later.

A tradition of the hills is incomparable, and as the years of youth are shot golden by deeds, their mountaineering is not surprisingly satisfied. Halcyon days indeed.

This I count as the ultimate test of my Braehead days: in my poor way I have made many happy. May the strength of hills always be theirs—and the long content.

After Braehead School closed I had a spell as County Adviser but this was an intolerable indoor, bureaucratic job and I had to find an escape. What was new, different and demanding enough to throw up "security" and launch off into the slog of freelance work? A walk over all the Munros became the return to sanity and the book I wrote about it, "Hamish's Mountain Walk" followed—a pattern of wandering and writing which has kept me busy since. Five years later came the "Groats End Walk." Both these stravaiging tramps were duly reported in The Scotsman *so are included here. The quest for something new led to the compiling (with a friend Martyn Berry) of the anthology "Speak to the Hills" a big collection of British and Irish mountain poems, all 20th century, to the more general "Poems of the Scottish Hills" and even a collection of some of my own poems, "Time Gentlemen" (all Aberdeen University Press). The Munro Walk has a lot to answer for! It was a venture made possible by a host of friends, both from home, and living in the Highlands. I would like to think that my writings contribute something to the appreciation (and preservation) of the finest heritage in the world.*

3. The Munro Marathon

TWO days of contrast: April 4 by the shore under Ben More in Mull saw the sun coming up in golden promise as it would do for weeks; deer crossed the road in the half light, a pheasant honked in the wood, a buzzard circled and mewed on the hill while from shore and sea came the mixed, subtle orchestration of waders, ducks and divers. The sounds of silence. The hills at their loveliest.

A few hours later we were perched 3169 feet up on Ben More. The compass on the summit is many degrees off true but on that day that was no worry. The girls lay sprawled in bikinis and the men bared pale torsos to the sun. It was very good.

One hundred and twelve days later, on July 24, two figures groped their way up Ben Hope, faces averted from the beating rain, plodding

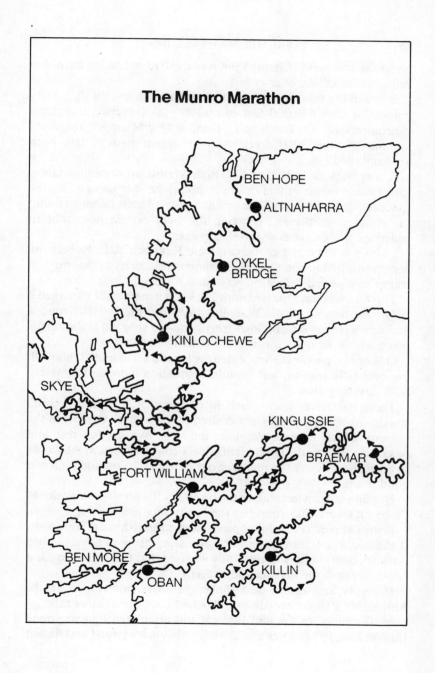

The Munro Marathon

BEN HOPE

ALTNAHARRA

OYKEL
BRIDGE

KINLOCHEWE

SKYE

KINGUSSIE

BRAEMAR

FORT WILLIAM

BEN MORE

KILLIN

OBAN

on to the trig point. Champagne was quaffed in the icy lee of the cairn, weeks of wet over at last.

Between the two days lay an unusual and unique "walk": 1639 miles of it with 449,000 feet of ascent—the traverse, in a single expedition, of all Scotland's, then, 279 "Munros" (separate mountains over 3000 feet). A long dream had at last been accomplished.

It was back in 1891 that Sir Hugh Munro produced his tables listing these magic mountains and though he was baulked by the Inaccessible Pinnacle on Skye he was a great pioneer of hill-bashing: the country gentleman, knowing the right people no doubt to penetrate those vast deer-forested ranges.

In 1901 a Reverend gentleman from Rannoch, A.E. Robertson, became the first to complete all the summits listed: by cycle, trap and tramp at a period before railways and surfaced roads.

This feat was not repeated until 1923 and a mere eight managed it before the Second World War. But 1970 saw the first 100 rounds and now a steady stream flows merrily on—a spur, an ambition for what is after all quite a ridiculous activity anyway.

One or two people even repeated the lot and at the end of this walk my own tally rose to four rounds, a situation more embarrassing than anything else.

There has never been much in the way of a "speed record" sought—something really not desired either, as alien to most of the reasons which take people into the hills. We go for rest and relaxation, to breathe purer air and walk empty spaces, in the words of Sir Robert Grieve "to recharge our batteries." You don't hurry a good dram.

Nor do you turn teetotal when you empty the bottle—so no doubt I'll be on to my fifth round of the heady mixture.

Being happiest on the hills I need few excuses to head off upwards. (I shamed a company recently by admitting never to have climbed Arthur's Seat—and was naturally accused that this was because it failed to reach the mystical 3000 feet.)

However, one last logical challenge did remain: to do all the Munros as a single expedition. This had been a persistent talking-point for years. In the mid 1960s it was attempted by two young English lads, fell-runners and climbers, they were strong and fit, but

Blackrock Cottage on Rannoch Moor with the Buachaille Etive Mor beyond

they eventually failed through trying to rush it. Dietary and other troubles forced these Ripley brothers to abandon the attempt.

Quite a few cross-country "treks" have been done going from North-South or East-West, often taking in many Munros en route. John Hinde had many RAF Kinloss Mountain Rescue teams doing such trips successfully and two years back Sandy Cousins walked from Cape Wrath to his home in Glasgow—370 miles with 47 Munros and 90,000 feet of ascent. But if these encourage, there were other woeful tales of failure on similar escapades.

Johnny and Sandy, of course, were experienced, all-round mountaineers, who already knew Scotland well, and anyone trying something like these trips through the Scottish hills without an already extensive background is risking failure, disappointment and even disaster. As a local once said of Liathach to W.H. Murray: "She is majestic, but she is not to be tampered with."

Before this expedition I used to call our weather "unpredictable," now I'm much more likely to call it "pernicious." Respect goes with one as close as a dog at heel. Hills are not neutral.

For the first 55 summits I had no rain: April blazing along in enervating heatwave; for the last three weeks I had no dry day and often faced lacerating storms. The landscape at times seemed intent on personal destruction. It could never be casually treated.

Previous knowledge was of great value in the planning—it took 18 months, from the day I looked at a map of Scotland and began to doodle a long thin line on it linking up those 279 summits, till the day I bade Mull farewell and headed off along the final line. On all but a dozen days I was alone (and how that sharpens awareness) but the whole expedition was backed by scores of helpers.

There were 42 caches along the way and it took much of February preparing them. I never want to tie another parcel in my life.

These were left with a fascinating variety of people: hoteliers, roadmen, shepherds, schoolteacher, doctor, wardens of hostels and camp sites, farmers, foresters, outdoor activity folk, railway linesmen, banker, toymaker—you name it.

A few were left in very remote spots, simply buried under cairns. They were often attacked by vermin, leaving only tins without labels to give odd surprise meals—like spinach and Nestle's cream. As well as this source of food, friends came up every weekend with fresh supplies—so altogether a great deal of work went into ensuring adequate feeding. I had no dreams or visions or gastronomic longings."

I also planned for at least one rest day a week, a scheme which followed not only human but divine wisdom. The days were long and hard (the average being 14½ miles and 4000 feet) and travelling light, there was little enough in reserve.

It had to be a disciplined, slow, steady progression—which to one of somewhat choleric disposition was very good for the soul no doubt.

Like a ship setting sail on a circumnavigation, once launched you are away, self-contained, wanting nothing. Few are lucky enough to escape the ties of everyday life and ascend their happiness. It was in many ways a humbling experience.

It was a crowded life, strangely, for all the incidents and action went into the day's walking (anything up to 15 hours of it). After that it was often a case of sealing oneself into the tent, like a hornbill, to cook and sleep while the rain and midges beat their frustration on the roof. Midges are no joke; I have seen fine streaking performed by innocent swimmers who knew not what they did; I have seen pedestrians cross the road to avoid a blotchy, bitten friend (muttering something the while about the infectious diseases hospital); I have seen strong men weep, and children cry.

A school lad was wailing from the tent next to mine in Skye once: "What will I do? What will I do? The tent's full of midges." From beyond another voice suggested: "Open the door and let them out." Which he did.

That "the long walk" was virtually a solo trip was not intentional—but without broadcasting widely there was no likely companion available and to a large extent the early plans were kept secret. The spice of competition saw to that—and also the wee nibbling fear of failure. There was also a sneaking desire for this solitude.

Over the last 20 years I've climbed something like 1500 Munros (even my poor dog's done 600), yet of the 279 listed only about 60 had been done alone.

Much of the time, too, those hill days had had the burden of responsibility. When one of my school lads first pointed out "a grey hair, sur"—I told him why. To go alone was a tonic. The constant demands of the trip would have made difficulties for a large party including the real dangers of squabbling from over-proximity for too long.

So after those days of spring joy on Mull, and two weeks of valley-level support for the Glencoe-Cruachan area, I wandered alone, circling through the Perthshire bumps to Tyndrum where Barclay Fraser from Cramond joined me with mail and food and new maps for the coming SW (Argyll) country.

Farewell to Barclay on Ben Lui. A canoe was used to reach Ben Lomond and eastwards at Strathyre, Robert Elton, another Scottish Mountaineering Club friend, met me—and brought the first rain of the route. Wild weather, snow and rain chased me north and east, Trans-Tay to the Tilt and on to the farthest east Munro, Mount Keen.

The Cairngorms led back to the A9 and various circuits from it. I used a cycle to cut down walking on this "death road"—and three times was ditched by mad motorists. It was a joy then to leave even the tent behind for a section called "Lochaber and back"; there was an abundance of bothies and good hostels.

The ten peaks of the Mamores gave the biggest haul in a day—but the Nevis-Aonachs-Grey Corries day in dramatic snow showers was better fun. Big days on the whole were not sought but here and on the Shiel ridges, Affric and a few other places they were naturally lined up, and logically/logistically best done in the day. Conservation of resources was always important.

Across the Great Glen the route became less complex: a slow northerly progression, zig-zagging back and forth along the predominantly east-west ridges. Into Knoydart: trouble from storm and running out of Gaz (Zip firelighters a messy substitute). Into Skye: where weather cleared and Peter Miller from Aberfeldy, at 17, had a first taste of rock mountains. Into heatwave fore massive days round Glen Shiel and Glen Affric. Then the last three weeks of woeful wind and rain.

The wildest storm of all was in the Assynt hills where I had the peculiar experience, while scrambling up a rock chimney, of being lifted off my holds and left poised in the updraught. Below, in the corries, the waterfalls were shooting up into the air.

The noise was fantastic. On the crest one crawled or lay gulping under pounding gusts—and all the time knowing speed mattered. The deluge would raise the rivers and a vital crossing lay below on the other side. It took three attempts before, thigh deep, the brown force was managed and the last eight miles of road plod in the rain could be tackled. The pipits rising from the heather were only able to fly backwards.

For the last two weeks I had low-level support from Mike Keates of Inverness—and when at last we'd supped our champagne and dined in style in Inverness, we dashed for Skye and the joys and contrasts of rock again. There, too, we met some of our local Braes o' Fife Mountaineering Club who had given the bulk of help before and during the trip.

For the statistically minded: 76 summits were obscured, people were encountered on 44 peaks, and on 100 days I was alone, accounting for 260 ascents. Ten hostels and ten climbing huts were used, seven nights were spent in hotels or friends' homes and 62 nights were spent under canvas (even above 3000 feet).

Equipment had to be light-weight. Very much Scottish in character it proved too. The vital items: tent, sleeping bag, waterproofs, rucksack and stove are where weight really counts. I managed never to carry as much as 30 pounds. A special tent (3½lb of it) was provided by Tulloch Mountaincraft. My sleeping bag was from Blacks and the rucksack a Tiso Special. I wore out two pairs of boots, holding them together with string and wire hopefully until the weekend supporters could replace them. Berghaus provided the vital waterproofs.

Years of lightweight camping had already pruned gear down to the lowest common denominator and I had few troubles or shortages. With an arthritic hip and a rheumatic shoulder I just cannot carry weight anyway.

So now it's all over. Friends back from the Alps concede that after all I may have something of an excuse for not being out there. Aye, indeed, more than ever I love my own land—its sweeping and often bewildering changes and challenges, its joys and delights, its incomparable peace and beauty.

We have a landscape unique in Europe. It is just a pity we do not have the political imagination and leadership to ensure its best survival. When the thousandth person has done the Munros, what will the hills be like then?

The challenge of walking John o' Groats to Land's End
is an obvious one but road-walking is not attractive to a
hill wanderer. I began to think of a mountain route and
slowly other reasons for going accumulated. Five years
after the Munro marathon sloth was finally overcome
and I took the dog off on a six-month walk.

4. A Groats End Walk

I left Fife quietly by train, and in its own inimitable way the system dropped me off at Wick in the summer dim. I walked out of the station wondering what to do and was at once offered a lift to Keiss. I took it, as it would place me an easy walk from my start at John o' Groats. I could camp somewhere overnight and the big walk could start on the morrow.

At Keiss I was dropped off. A wind seemed to be coming directly from the North Pole and I could only just make out the glow of street lights through the driving snow. I groped about a bit and then stumbled on some brighter lights: the Sinclair Bay Hotel. I went in, thankfully, for bed and breakfast—and, more immediately, some tea and a dram.

Snug in bed, I watched the snow drive past the window and chuckled. Things were happening even before I reached the starting line. The next morning I caught a bus to John o' Groats and walked out to Duncansby Head before turning west. For the next nine days it snowed off and on.

On Ben Hope, our most northerly 3000-ft summit, the snow was feet deep and I wished I had my skis. To break up on to its summit plateau from the east I had to cut steps and break through a cornice using a section of tent pole. The camp at 2000 feet looked like something in the Arctic.

Yet only a few days later, at normally grim Cape Wrath, my tent was reflected in a peaty pool while I sat outside to watch a rainbow sunset down the coast to Sandwood Bay. A few days later again I woke to peer out the tent because I could hear peregrines calling nearby—and there was mighty Suilven plastered in new snow.

It was not really the start I had envisaged, or geared up for, but I would not have missed it for anything. My appreciation of Scotland's wilderness has been deepened by absence.

34

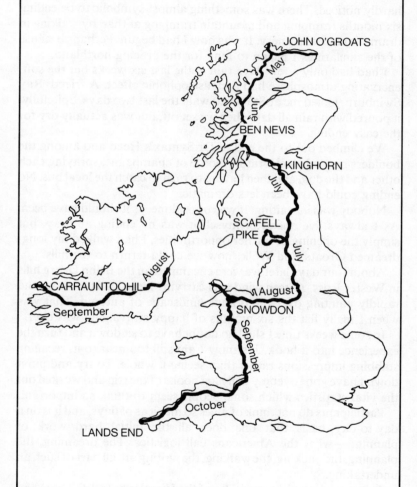

**The Groats End
Walk Route**

JOHN O'GROATS

May

June

BEN NEVIS

KINGHORN

July

SCAFELL
PIKE

July

CARRAUNTOOHIL

September

August

SNOWDON

September

October

LANDS END

The north coast of Devon and Cornwall has some majestic cliff scenery and an abundance of sandy bays on a par with Sandwood in Sutherland.

Towns like Newquay, with their summer urban crowds were hardly noticed. There was something almost symbolic to be ending six months tramping and mountain tramping at that, by walking in dramatic coastal scenery. It was how I had begun. Perhaps because of the similarities I began to long for the bracing northland.

I had had only a few days rain in the last six weeks but the soft, enervating atmosphere had a claustrophobic effect. A friend, Ray Swinburn, joined me at St Ives to walk the last two days. Spitefully, it poured with rain all day when we set off, but was actually dry for the easy ending.

We climbed out to the end of Dr Syntax's Head and among the boulders opened a celebratory bottle of champagne, spraying each other and the dog, and then having to rush to catch the local bus. No ending could have been less dramatic.

Nobody was in waiting. It was ours alone, as it should have been. As I always live ahead of myself it was no ending anyway, but simply the opening of further opportunities. I had walked my long-dreamed Groats End Walk: now we could return to the hills.

About four days later we were encamped on the Beinn Dearg hills in Wester Ross. A keen wind was carrying large loads of snow and rapidly painting over the orange landscape of autumn. That was when I really felt the six months of happy stravaiging was over.

In some weeks time I shall no doubt have to sit down and turn the experience into a book. Just now I am still too near to it, recalling stabbing impressions rather than seeing it whole. To try and pin it down I have gone over my daily log books of the trip and worked out the vital statistics which some people seem to think so important.

Participants do not think of miles so much as of days, and it is on a day-to-day basis that one does all the initial hard work of planning—what the Americans call logistics. The dreaming, the planning, the packing, the walking, the writing are all part of such an undertaking.

This week I am showing slides of the Himalayas (a 1977 trip) and have a meeting to discuss ideas for a ploy in 1982. A long expedition, of any kind, is an excellent means of putting "time" back into a subservient position. Without our dreams the daily round would be mere drudgery. And, oh, the joy when we lock the office and set off to put feet to our dreams.

Let me enumerate what I got up to those months away. I was walking from May 2 until October 23—175 days, of which 29 were actually not spent walking. The 146 walking days covered 2500 miles and gave 250,000 feet of ascent, an average of 17 and 1700. It broke down:

(1) The north coast walk already mentioned;

(2) a north-south walk over 33 Munros from Ben Hope to Ben Lomond, keeping to really remote areas on the way;

(3) with Ray Swinburn, walking the way of the line of the coming West Highland Way, that rather unnecessary creation of the bureaucrats;

(4) completing a sixth round of our daft Munro game;

(5) a canoe run down the River Forth from Loch Ard to Kinghorn, home;

(6) a walk through the Borders, a fine mix of wee hills and history to link with

(7) the walkers' M1 of the Pennine Way, from which I diverted to the Lakes for

(8) the English 3000ders and for (9) the three country summits (only walked a handful of times to date);

(10) coast-to-coast across Ireland from Dun Laoghaure to Dingle taking in (11) the Irish 3000ders and (12) the first-ever walking link between the four country summits: Ben Nevis, Scafell Pike, Snowdon and Carrauntoohil; (13) the Welsh 3000ders; (14) a north-south traverse of the Welsh hills: Snowdonia, Rhinogs, Cader Idris, Plynlimon, the Rhaedor hills, Brecon Beacons, Black Mountains and down the Wye by the Offa's Dyke Footpath;

(15) the south-west hills and Coastal Path; Mendips, Quantocks, Brendons, Exmoor, etc. to (16) finaly sew then all together with John o' Groats to Land's End completed.

Perhaps I shall gain an entry in some book of records—for the slowest, most devious linking of those two over-exposed ends of the Isles. My only justification is that it was done for fun.

The cynic might also argue it was done for financial gain, but this is, alas, a fallacy. It is unlikely that writing about it will come anywhere near covering the costs.

No, it is a fun thing first and last, and one of my concerns from what I saw during the trip is that some of the fun is being taken out of our hill game—by interfering busy bodies, however well-meaning by the planners and bureaucrats who feel we are all incapable of doing anything unless it is all done for us, by commercial interests and gear manufacturers who would have us priced off our hills, by the educationists offering their synthetic "simulated adventure." It is an alarming picture. It is beginning to happen in Scotland. We may yet be protected out of our own.

I had my Sheltie, Storm, with me and could not have asked for a better companion, but then he is an admirably well behaved dog both on the hills and in hotels which we had to use occasionally. There are dogs and dogs, just as there are people and people, and it only needs a few minutes in their presence to form opinions (ask any shepherd).

I think the longest time we were apart was on the boat from Holyhead to Dun Laoghaire, and he came out from his cage there having collected fleas which then would appear publicly in all the wrong places. On landing I was mis-directed and did a two-hour walk to a cousin's house which was really only quarter of an hour away. Then when I arrived I found it all locked up as she was away on holiday. A very Irish welcome.

I was then grilled in a heatwave for the longest spell I ever had on road-walking which I hate, before the "monsoon" in the west found us.

To be fair, Carrauntoohil was the only one of the four highest country summit to give a view, and the only one on which there was nobody else present. The other country summits crawled with people and are really soiled and revolting urban extensions in the summer.

The summit of Ben Nevis is long overdue for a real clean-up to bury all the remains, cairns, litter and vain monuments and signs of silly human visits. No other animal fouls its environment like homo sapiens.

We are losing the earth we love. In each country I saw intrusive nuclear power stations (not in Ireland, where peat is providing 40 per cent) and we are going to be trampled into this all over the place, leaving an inheritance of unknown dangers and desolation to our children.

The Flodden Memorial in Selkirk, one of the finest of the many Border monuments

It is a picture of gloom, and I saw nothing on my look about our island to encourage me. I am sure that all this is part of the reason why people go to the hills. It is grand escapism. And in a European sense our Scottish wilderness is one of the vital escapes to sanity.

I have long loved the Irish hills, for they are in many ways looking as ours might have done had we not had a history of clearances for sheep or deer. Their hills rise out of a patchwork of green fields, stitched with hedgerows, hazed with turf reek and buttoned with the white gleam of homes.

I have stood on Galtymore and heard the laughter of children in the plains below. Even the remote parts are still lived in. It is a peopled landscape while ours is a selfishly created desert, assuming we can have wet deserts.

I may have started across Ireland in a heatwave, but on Brandon, our Isles' most westerly 3000-footer, I had a 16-hour "shower." I finally pitched the tent at 2000 feet, with midges out in force, crawled in thankfully—and then discovered I had pitched it on top of an ants' nest.

Once back on my real line for Land's End, Ireland having been a diversion to do the country summits, I had only half a dozen really wet and miserable days. Wales was to give a traverse which was one of the highlights of the journey. It was largely new ground to me and it was breathtakingly beautiful in a way no cataloguing of the poetic names above can convey.

It was past the tourist season; the people were friendly and hospitable, the colours flushing up to the first frosts—delightful. Even the book collector in me had its fling at Hay-on-Wye, which has more bookshops than any town in the world. It is the town's main industry and, being a far cry from Edinburgh, the prices of Scottish items were temptingly reasonable.

I sometimes read while walking on roads, a habit which has landed me in more than one ditch but fills the hours of inescapable roadbashing of which England has its share. Frequently I tried cross-country lines of rights-of-way which are marked on the maps only to meet barriers of brambles, nettles and hawthorn. I reckon England is going to loose most of her rights-of-way by neglect.

The "official" paths of the south-west coast and Offa's Dyke therefore have an important place. Navigation is far more difficult through farmland than over the hills—which is why they may need such paths and ways, and why Scotland does not.

There is nothing to stop anyone walking our West Highland Way, now, without making a set piece of it. It is not in the Scottish tradition, but as we are largely dominated by English-copying or trained bureaucrats we are foisted with alien conceptions whether we want them or not.

The mountains are not to be tamed by decree, and the creation of any mountain routes would be highly irresponsible. If people are not capable of going on the hill unaided, then the aid is misplaced. We do not want the hills prostituted, and the bureaucratic pimps need to be told where to get off.

The Pennine Way is now in many places a worn, foul mud track because of the magic appeal artificially stimulated by its special designation. It is a great route, in fact, one to wander slowly, stravaiging at its best, to see many things of interest, but it is seldom done for interest.

Going north-south I had it largely to myself because the guide books all go south-north and the sheep all follow. During one hour each day I would meet the mobs jostling north and then have it to myself again.

It was being used by the ton-up kids to swell their egos. Many were incapable of travelling without a transistor blaring all the time. And this is what we are introducing to the bonny banks and the inner reaches of Corrie Ba. Are we all daft?

At lower levels I am not against such paths. In fact, I would rather like to see them all linked up to make a Land's End to John o' Groats Walkway. A bit by the Severn and a link by canal towpaths like those I used going to Wales to Edale would be needed in England, and in Scotland a link through the Borders to join Loch Lomond, while there is an almost completed route up the Great Glen and the north-east coast that would be a fine finish, balancing the south-west of Devon and Cornwall.

I was in Morocco to ski, climb and trek for the three months before this escapade, so the packing was done in a rush. I made one delivery run to Sutherland and back to leave caches and climb a few stray Munros for the sixth time (the rest were on the route and were done in determined fashion though I did skip many others due to some wild weather. I am no slave to a plan.

I sent off huge parcels to Sheffield (where I had a few days and did the posting for Wales), to Ruthin (ditto for the south-west) and Dublin. Something like 70 maps were used, hundreds of films and all the many things needed to keep in the field. Even the dog's Frolic packets totalled up to my body weight. The actual work for this journey was every bit as complex and demanding as for an expedition to the Himalayas. Ah, if we could only eat heather . . .

The route was never something I felt bound to. I had a rough timetable and walked off to see Britain's hills and so enrich my experience therein. To make things bend to suit a walk I feel is contrary to nature and takes its toll. We must bend to nature, bowing to the wind and treading softly in the wilderness. I am always after willy-wispy interests anyway.

I would not do this trip again, for though I enjoyed it, especially the hilly parts, too much of it was simply in farming country. Put it this way: why walk the fields of pretty Somerset when you could be walking the splendour of far Sutherland?

Happily it is far to Sutherland, and there is still some real wilderness, yet even in the English or Welsh hills, as soon as I left the beaten track I hardly ever met anyone. There is a deal of magnificent wild country in Wales, no matter how lapped it is by the millions of England. Basically ninety per cent of tourists never go farther than half a mile from their cars. This walk was a conscious breaking out from our encapsulated society.

Though done largely alone I am no loner. Several times friends did join me, sometimes even for weeks, but for the simple, smooth running of such a big venture being alone removes a host of complications. Going alone heightens the experience, too, is not more dangerous (you take more care) and leaves you completely free of pressure.

My one companion, Storm, did not complain once. My *Hamish's Mountain Walk* has brought me many letters, not necessarily from hard climbers or walkers, and I feel that this, too, is a tale to be told which all can read.

This is something we all associate with. It is about here and now—not some super-feat on a far and unpronounceable peak in

Darien—so I am glad to share it. I had a marvellously happy time personally, but the joy was edged with concern: "... to travel is despair, for men are foolish, everywhere."

*Half way through the Braehead days I inherited fathers'
dog Kitchy: a Shetland Collie of chacter who eventually
became the school's expedition mascot, protector and
friend. He must have been up about two thousand hills in
his life and it did not seem possible that another dog
could take his place, but one did. His name is Storm.*

5. Top Dog, Storm

RECENTLY circumstances took me to Ireland for several
weeks without my dog, Storm. In the tent, on the hill,
passing ice-cream machines, I kept reacting as if he were
there. He usually is, for I have never been owned by a dog
before.

In Mitchelstown, under the Galtymore Hills, I particularly
remember one incident of the Irish coast-to-coast walk Storm and I
had made some years earlier. We had been sitting on a bench in the
main square when a blind girl was led towards us by an older
woman. The woman asked if the girl could "touch the dog so as to
see him." The child's hands played awhile over the soft coat of the
Sheltie and then she stood up with a sigh and a smile: "Sure, he's a
gorgeous fella." It was a rather moving incident—but she was right,
he is a gorgeous fella.

Storm came to me in a fashion which was made for romantic
fiction and I hestitate to describe it. After the long years with Kitchy
we had no heart for another dog. Old Kitchy had had a stroke when
a puppy jumped on him unexpectedly and just slowly faded away.
(The Siamese cat climbed in beside him and did likewise.) I was in
Morocco and this double sadness was kept from me—except the
vet's bill was addressed to Mr Brown and was sent on. Life without a
dog was incomplete but how could we follow such a character as
Kitchy?

Motoring home from Morocco the following year I stopped to
look at Rosslyn Chapel and a woman passed with two Shetland
sheepdogs. They were beauties (not the weird midgets now so
fashionable) and I rushed after her to find their source. The nearby
kennels she mentioned had nothing available but gave me a Fife
contact. They had nothing either but promised to phone when there

44

Storm, during the Lochinver - Berriedale walk

were puppies available. Nothing happened and months later I rang them. They apologised but their bitch had "missed." We chatted a bit and then the woman said they did have a two-year-old they should part with, being a bit too big for a stud dog or for winning top prizes in the show ring, and with six Shelties the house was fully occupied. Would I be interested in an adult dog?

Would I not! We had procrastinated partly because of the difficulty of fitting in the time needed for the training of a puppy so to gain one which was house-trained, had all its medical needs covered and was show-ring obedient seemed too good to be true. I drove over at once to meet Storm.

The room I was shown in to had six Shelties milling about but one solemn charmer came up and put his head on my knees to be petted. "Which is Storm?" I asked. "He's the one who seems to have chosen you," was the reply. How true this was for, friendly though he is with a circle of friends, neighbours and relatives, he is utterly my dog or, rather vice-versa, for he initiated the relationship!

I am no doggy sentimentalist, let me add, but I do believe a trained obedient, pleasant dog can be a delight in any home and I'd hate to be without one

Storm sat on the front seat as I drove home, with a very "solemn" expression, which is one of his characteristics, and I wondered what lay ahead. I rang the front door and left him there for mother to find. "Oh no!" she gasped, but was soon enrolled as Number Two Human.

It took Storm a while to realise he did not have to walk one inch from my ankles all the time (a most unnatural progression) and he exploded into a belated acquaintance with the world. He curiously was, and is, boundless and this allied to a soft nature makes him safe with wildlife. As a constant hill companion he had to learn, at once, that sheep were to be left alone. That only took a weekend but it started with an embarrassing incident.

We travelled down to the Borders (I wanted to see the then near-complete Meggat Dam) and we slept near it in my caravanette so I could take photographs in the morning light. We went out first thing to water some grass tussocks. Storm was free first and just then some sheep ambled past. Not having seen sheep before he was curious and walked over to them. They moved off. He followed. In seconds they were scampering off with Storm following. Simultaneously I saw what was happening and yelled—and a Land Rover came round the track.

Thank goodness it was driven by an understanding shepherd. He didn't just see a dog chasing sheep but a dog who came to heel, instantly on command. "You'll have no trouble training that one," he noted. We had a crack about dogs and humans in general and he summed things up with "I wish people just had the intelligence of dogs; a bad dog is only what his master makes him."

That day Storm received several warnings and two punishments and has never looked at a sheep since. On the hill now I know there will be sheep ahead because Storm will come back to heel automatically. We can walk through farmyards or anywhere without worry. The only time he goes on a lead is when I need to protect him from idiot humans driving motor cars. A trained dog is a great companion, an untrained dog is a menace and my sympathies lie entirely with long-suffering farmers and shepherds. "It's not the bad dogs we should shoot; it's their owners!"

Naturally, Kitchy having done so, I wanted to see Storm round all the Munros and this took five or six years to accomplish. It led me to a ridiculous seventh round in the passing and at times our interests conflicted. Before completing the Scottish 3,000ders Storm had already been over the English, Welsh and Irish "threes" linking them in the six month, continuous walk from John o' Groats to Lands End, the story told in *Hamish's Groats End Walk*. He has visited Ireland on several occasions but his first hours on Irish soil were pantomime.

He had been caged on the ferry across from Holyhead (we had no vehicle) and when we landed I asked directions for a cousin's house and we were cheerfully sent off in the wrong direction. An hour later we sat wearily with a curry carry-out on the church wall in Dun Laoghaire (where we'd started) when the church doors opened and hundreds of people streamed out. Across the water this might have been an embarrassing situation but not in Ireland.

A dozen men were soon arguing as to how I should reach my destination. One man produced the comment "Jasus, you can't get there from here." When we did reach the house it was empty. Kind neighbours took us in for tea until the key came (my cousin had gone off to Galway) and in the middle of nibbling *barn brack* I noticed a flea on Storm's coat. I grabbed this and for the next hour sat with a clenched fist . . .

Near the start of that long hike I'd been involved in a radio programme with Alistair Hetherington and Gordon Adam and was "interviewed" in the hotel at Scourie. Storm was tied to a stool out of the way and the recording commenced. Storm spotted his food dish and went for it only to find he was leashed. He tugged, the stool squealed across the linoleum and a paw sent the tin dish clattering. "Who needs a sound effects department? Let's start again."

He has starred in several bits of filming for TV and in Bristol a good scene was set up and rehearsed in a park above the Avon. Storm was to appear and, at a call, run across and leap up into my arms. He did this several times perfectly then, when the cameras were rolling, his dash stopped abruptly at an intervening tree and he stood against it on three legs. I'd swear he was grinning!

His leaping into my arms at a bidding had its more practical side on difficult terrain such as the Cuillin Ridge but even there, frequently, when I thought he would need assistance, he would appear *above* the problem part, having found his own way round. Like Kitchy he seemed to love the rough rockiness of the Cuillin. There were times when he went on a long lead to ease my apprehensions, not his, such as the time he chose to roll in the snow on the summit of Am Basteir—as exposed a place as you can find.

Most of his Cuillin Munros were done in winter conditions. He has an asset in owning built-in crampons, but for the Inaccessible Pinnacle he went into the rucksack, and I half-climbed and was half-hauled up the verglas-plastered short side courtesy of an army team. His head was poking out and at a scrabbling moment of difficulty he gave my ear an encouraging lick.

He is never depressed, always cheerful and "rarin' to go," never girns, eats anything (his or anyone else's) and is quite impossible to live up to. There are dog worlds we know nothing about. How, for instance, does he know that the rucksack is being packed for Morocco, or this recent Irish trip, in which he is not involved—as against other trips where he is going as well? He can tell, days ahead, and the reproachful looks I receive during a foreign packing would

melt a heart of stone. He is happy enough when I'm away but the
welcome back is always ecstatic.

Their world of scent is one we know nothing about. I'm sure if he
were lost in the Highlands he'd follow his nose home. Places, many
places, are recognised by scent. In the car he will sit with his nose to
the air intake with a look of bliss on his face at times: high on scents.
A squirrel a quarter of a mile up the road will cause him to stand up
waiting for a sighting. He will nose out grouse in the heather just for
the hell of startling them into the air, and a change from them usually
giving me heart-failure.

Squirrels, he thinks, are cheats. When he wants to play with them
they will run up trees! (The first time he was six feet up a big pine
before he realised he was not equipped for trees.) He is willing to be
friends with all things but cats do not always understand this as
scars on his nose testify. I see a great deal of wildlife thanks to his
more efficient senses. Even in the caravanette I am frequently woken
at unearthly hours by his wildlife watching from our "hide." On
Papa Stour he was quite happy to meet bonxie chicks nose-to-beak
but not so keen on the attacks of the parent birds and I made sure he
did not approach too close to the fulmar chicks.

He has been to many interesting corners, some of them
approached by canoe, a form of transport of whch he thoroughly
approves yielding as it does diving gannets, puffin antics, porpoises
playing and camp sites on wild and lonely strands. He is bigger and
heavier than Kitchy, and I'm a decade older, so I'm not so keen on
him in my rucksack. The first time nearly had fatal consequences.

We made a round trip into Glen Affric, starting from Loch Duich
and finishing at Cluanie where the bike had been left to help us down
the long glen. As we sped down, I was aware of Storm's head peering
over my shoulder and thought this must look odd to anyone coming
towards us. A bus was grinding up the road and I saw the driver give
a startled "double take" as we passed. He was so busy looking back
at us that he took his bus halfway up the grass bank.

We set out last Christmas-Hogmany to finish off our respective
Munro rounds and early in the year came south of the Great Glen to
Nancy Smith's private hostel at Fersit beside Loch Treig to organise
a sortie into the hills south of Loch Laggan. These, strangely, have
no collective name but Ben Alder is the dominant summit. Storm

wanted the four Munros on the other side of the Bealach Dubh from Ben Alder. I went along as his chef and porter.

Beinn a' Chlachair (which sounds like the name of a single malt) was climbed on the way in and before reaching Culra Bothy we left the rucksack to add Carn Dearg as well, which is very much an eastern tail peak to the main body of Storm's ridge of peaks. That left three, which we planned to traverse to exit from their western end. The bothy was dank from heavy use over Hogmanay and a gang of Fife lads and I preferred to stand and blether outside under a crisp, starry sky. Storm, inside, gave their frying pan a good clean. (Our local club had soon learnt not to leave any food at floor level— unless they actually want a burnt dixi cleaned!).

In the morning it was snowing and we tramped the miles up to the Bealach Dubh with all the icy patches disguised by the new powdering. We both had some exciting slides. The pass was bleak, with the mist down and the wind moaning in the sad wreckage of a crashed aeroplane.

Geal Charn, our first hill, cumulates in a featureless plateau and to ensure we actually found the summit cairn we first wandered up to the summit of Lancet Edge, so we could take an accurate bearing over the wasteland miles.

We had two miles to go over complex country yet the cairn loomed out of the gloom as and where expected. It had to—50 yards on there was a sneering edge of cornice.

Two swooping drops and ascents on the grand highway of ridge took us over Aonach Beag (there isn't an Aonach Mor) to Beinn Eibhinn *the beautiful hill,* an appropriate place for Storm's 277-up. He promptly anointed it!

Storm had come a long way from his restrictive years as a show dog. It appals me that so called dog-lovers can go in for genetic engineering and the sort of slavery the show ring entails.

After the *Groats End Walk* book came out I showed Storm's previous owner the book. On the cover Storm sits with Snowdon behind him and she turned to her boss (owner of Storm's brother) showing him this and saying, "Isn't he grand? You'd never think he's had a broken leg as a puppy," which was the first I'd heard about that. He came with the name Storm. Imagine yelling his pedigree name on a misty hillside: Ellenyorn Spider's Web!

One day at Montrose three of us, who had just walked across Scotland without our dogs (it was lambing time), were exercising our reunited and excited trio on the sands. Their names were probably a fair comment on our crossing: Storm (Sheltie), Cloud (Springer) and Misty (German Shepherd).

Storm is very hard to live up to, but I suppose I can bask in his reflected glory. So often we are accosted on the hills with "Hello, you must be Hamish Brown" and, before the vain human could respond, the let-down follows, "Yes, we recognised the dog"! Storm can be guaranteed to steal the show, every time. Bearded hikers are ten a penny; there is only one Storm and, sure, he is a gorgeous fella.

SCOTTISH PLACES

*While most of this book has Scottish connections one
way or another the next half dozen pieces are concerned
with specific areas and places: Lowland hills, Highland
hills and Islands. It is a random selection for you can no
more pour all Scotland into six cups that you can a quart
into a pint bottle.*

6. The Pentland Seven

I wonder if Edinburgh folk realise how lucky they are having
hills on their doorstep? The Pentlands sprawl like a tame lion,
nuzzling into the town as if to try and draw attention to itself.
"Come and Play!" they plead.

It was the time of the Open Golf tournament at St Andrews—that
hot spell. It was revoltingly hot in town. An evening stroll round
Malleny Gardens (NTS), at Balerno showed it was equally
oppressive in the open. The only way to enjoy the hills would be to go
early. The dog and I departed at 5.30 on Saturday morning to make
a 15-mile round trip I had long planned.

Normally round trips are a bit artificial, dictated by the necessity
of returning to a car rather than suiting the natural landscape. The
round of the Seven Reservoirs proved to be satisfying in every
way—one of the best walks to be made in the Pentland Hills.

The early start not only saved me from being smitten by the sun
but it yielded a richer variety of wildlife and until the last hour the
only other people I saw were fishermen.

Torduff Reservoir was our first water, reached easily enough
from Colinton. It is a secretive lochan in the fold behind Torphin Hill
and is twinned with Clubbiedean Reservoir, which I skirted to the
south to see the earthworks shown on the map. These proved to be a
series of arcs, walls and ditches, cutting off an area by the lochan, a
good example of prehistoric defences.

We walked along by the Kinleith and Harlaw Farms, a road that
divided the sheeplands and the sown. The plains below were golden
with ripening grain but the landscape was still held together by many
trees. (We must never lose our trees as they have in parts of England).

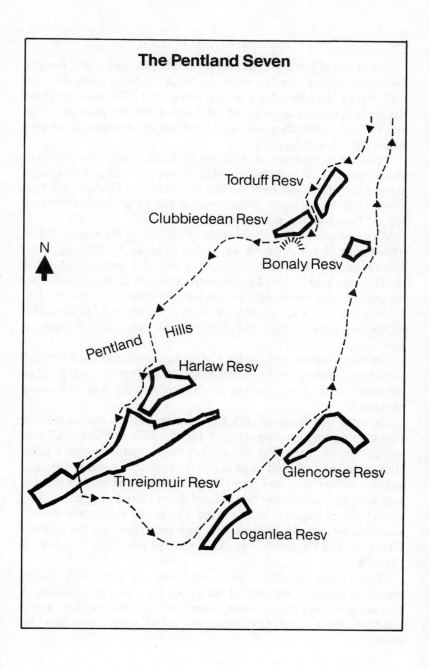

The Pentland Seven

Torduff Resv

Clubbiedean Resv

Bonaly Resv

N

Pentland Hills

Harlaw Resv

Threipmuir Resv

Glencorse Resv

Loganlea Resv

The Water of Leith with its villages of Balerno, Currie and Juniper Green lay largely invisible below us. Walking down there the view sadly lacks the hills which ranged to our left. The Kinleith Burn descends through the tangle of the Poet's Glen, the poet being the weaver poet Jamie Thomson, who lived in a cottage west of the glen called Mount Parnassus.

Harlaw Reservoir was surrounded by Scots pines, rather drilled in their ranks, but a definite aesthetic improvement. Threipmuir Reservoir, which was only feeding a trickle into Harlaw, has had several areas verging it planted with a mix of deciduous trees so should be attractive in time.

We came out at Red Moss Reserve (SWT), at the boggy end of Threipmuir and suddenly it was a day of birds. Moorhens, coots, blackheaded gulls, a heron and many ducks were all loud in the shifting mist and a pair of grebes were wrapped up in each other as we passed over the bridge for the beech avenue to Bavelaw. The farmlands, with four reservoirs, were abruptly left as the road climbed up between the brave trees that link rich valley and sparser hills.

The mist was down to the level of the top fields and I just hoped I would hit off the gap of Green Cleuch. Sheep loomed out, large as elephants in the mist, and the dog's coat and my feet were soon saturated.

The mist was thick enough I had to dig out the compass for a check. Once into the deep cleft of the dry valley of Green Cleuch navigation was easy. The waterfall of the Logan Burn was a mere trickle. Beside it camped some youngsters with bikes and belongings scattered about and unwashed dixies sitting in the burn. Someone was snoring! Storm, my dog, helped clean their frying pan.

The clouds began to shift on Scald Law, the Pentland's highest summit, and it gradually cleared as we wended our way to Loganlee Reservoir and Glencorse Reservoir, the pair that lie in the heart of the hills.

Martins flew overhead, pipits and wagtails were busy, rooks passed in ragged flocks, ducks sat out on the water and families of dippers were busy on the burns. A hundred tiny fish scattered at my shadow and a huge green frog did an Olympic leap into the burn.

Just before turning up into the hills again we came on some geese in the roadside field. One flew out but the younger ones rushed about and jammed their heads in the fence. I had to lift them over. They waddled across the road and belly-flopped into the waters of Glencorse Reservoir. This reservoir was built in 1822 and Hugh Millar, who should have known, gave it high praise, comparing it with a genuine Highland loch. A church, founded in the time of Robert the Bruce, was submerged in creating the reservoir.

Suddenly it was hot and I dripped and drooped up to the gap between Harbour Hill and Capelaw where a salvation wind blew on us. Suddenly Edinburgh lay in sight again, impressively down. The Pentlands are not big hills, but they can give a good imitation.

Bonaly Reservoir was our odd seventh water of the round and all too soon we were descending the ravine edge back to the hot streets of the city. The Gas Works at Granton were the most obvious feature, but the eye of faith could pick out many features leading away to the Forth Bridge, the busy estuary and the Fife Lomonds in the heat haze.

Bonaly Tower is the welcome of the hills, the home created by Lord Cockburn after he married in 1811 and so often mentioned in the racy "Memorials of His Times." He was a Pentlands enthusiast, but who, living on their fringes, is otherwise?

7. *Rannoch Moor*

THE Blackmount road has always been the place where I consciously feel back home in "the house of the hills." The pass above Tyndrum acts as the porch, by Loch Tulla one receives a glimpse west of some of the majestic furnishings, but it is after those curving steps bear the traveller up on to The Moor that it dawns on one that this is no ordinary dwelling place—but a palace. There is even a page standing at the door.

This is the Rannoch Rowan. It stands west of the road, a thousand feet above sea level, potted, as it were, in a cloven boulder which allowed a casual seed to grow unmolested by the teeth of deer. I first spotted it when it was a seedling and, as I was then just a boy, we must be of an age, this sturdy tree and less-sturdy me. Salute it friends as you drive past. It is a tree of good fortune.

The Moor of Rannoch is one of those places which people either like or dislike at once. It has a crying loneliness which can panic people used to urban clatter and bustle. (I have seen it happen). It has a wind-wide spaciousness which can captivate all who desire the empty place of quietude (I have seen that happen, too). I was captured as a youth and make no apologies for a love confessed and an enthusiasm endorsed by experience.

Rannoch Moor is not a tame place. You dwell with it as you would with a tiger, in a respectful neutrality; but aware that the finest beast may become a man-eater at a quirk of fate or, more likely, through the stupidity of man. Man has never really won over The Moor.

Roads have successively cut lines across it on the west, the railway edges it on the east and a track of sorts crosses the northern part. Within that there is "a great deal of nothing," that most priceless asset. I will always remember, with dismay, how the pylons that were finally marched, in ugly array, to Skye, were placed on a route by the planners "because there was nothing there." Of course, "nothing there" means nothing of the material junk associated with man and his despoiling tactics. There is plenty of wildlife and an abundant beauty, a beauty that ranges from sweeping grandeur (a newly-painted skyscape perhaps) to intimate, tiny, perfection (a dewdrop in a leaf of lady's mantle).

Man has had his place there. It is a long time ago now for the signs

56

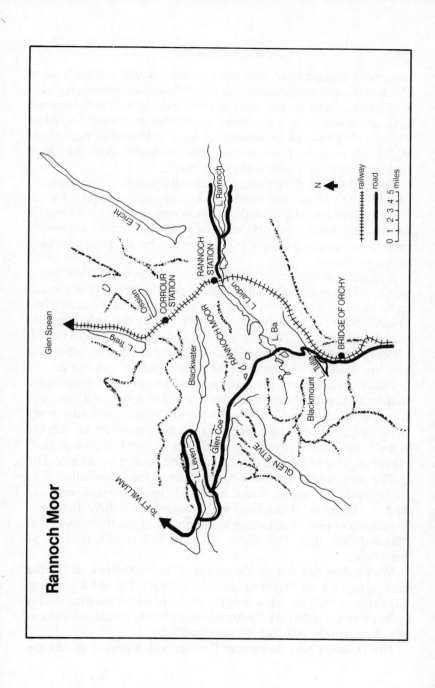

Rannoch Moor

are merely grassed-over ruins and a vivid green that patches a sober cloak of brown heather and black bog. What camp sites such places make: haunted by history and quiet below the stars. The quick-eyed may see a notice by the railway track that proclaims "Soldiers' Trenches." This was an attempt at land reclamation in the mid-eighteenth century. I wonder how the Redcoats liked the clarty moor? It was not a successful experiment.

The white roots of old trees stick out of the peat in many places. At one time The Moor was timbered. At Crannach and round Loch Tulla and up some side glens the last decaying remnants still struggle to survive, while on islets in the lochs on the moor there are woods that thrive simply because the destroying beasts have less easy access to them.

If I first found my way on to The Moor as a lad it was while taking parties of school pupils out regularly over a decade that I really came to know it intimately. We criss-crossed it in all directions. We skied and climbed the perimeter hills. We linked its lochs by canoe—and skated them too. We hunted the unique Rannoch Rush (which only has two sites in Europe). We studies the birds of the wilds. We saw the sweep of the seasons and knew sunshine and storm.

Because we were not car-orientated in those groups we also came to have a great affection for the railway. When it was built there was a gap of 30 miles, from Bridge of Orchy to Tulloch, that had nobody living in it. Stations apart it has not changed much and it was the railway company who built the road from Rannoch Station to Loch Rannoch. It was no accident that the line opened on August 11.

The construction engineers had to face all the inconveniences of moor travel—distance, water and peat. Great trenches were dug and all the till from the cuttings was swallowed cheerfully. In the end thousands of tons of ash wood were brought in and the railway was "floated" on this. The slight rise and fall is still noticed by travellers.

We used to visit the station master, Charles Murray, at Gorton and be regaled with tea and tales of the Moor. He had a conning-tower for viewing the line across the moor. In winter thawing out the points was a regular task. "After an hour of that I would come in and stand my frozen coat behind the door."

Not far away was Rowantree Cottage which made a good base.

The Rannoch Rowan in the 60's—still the Blackmount's welcoming gesture to the wilds of Rannoch Moor

Alas, it has been destroyed. I remember one party there running short of bread and a lad was dispatched on the morning "up train" to Tyndrum to buy supplies. This took little time and when he was seen hanging about in the cold with hours to the "down train" he was given a lift in a big new diesel pulling alumina tankers to Fort William. The sound of the train stopping outside the bothy brought us to the door. Our wee messenger climbed down, hung from the ladder, and dropped to the ground. He stood back and gave a saluting wave—and the huge train moved off once more. He is now a big, middle-aged man. I wonder if he remembers?

It was during this winter past that the Moor demonstrated its traditional temper to a friend and me. We wanted to climb some hills around Loch Ossian and these can be reached only by train—or by a long walk in. We packed up camp and drove to Bridge of Orchy Station only to find the train had gone through ten minutes before our "guestimate". We, therefore, just put it off 24 hours to save repacking and went for a day on the hills. It was so mild we were in shirt sleeves and had mini wellies on our feet. To save a long drive to Aviemore when we came out we drove over The Moor and round by Spean Bridge to go in from Tulloch Station. We had a pleasant night in Nancy Smith's independent hostel at Fersit: a cosy spot for a wet night which relented and pinned stars to the ceiling. We made sure of the train.

As it chuntered in bottom gear up along Loch Treig the sky in the west took on a sullen darkness. Snow was on its way. "Showers" was what the forecast had said. We descended at lonely Corrour Station and while Charles headed west for a summit he wanted to tick off in his Munros Tables, I had to take the dog up Beinn na Lap for one he wanted. It's hell being owned by a Munro-bagging dog.

Halfway up I heard a train coming and sat to watch it caterpillar its way across the black and white landscape. It was a goods heading north and as it passed over Corrour Summit you could almost hear its relief at heading downhill again. I lost it in the first flurry of snow.

It was an annoying climb. On the lower slopes the crust would not bear my weight and higher up we had cloud and snow so there was no view. The long, easy-angled ridge seemed to go on for ever even with the snow on our backs. At the cairn I donned crampons (the dog's are built in) and took the steepest, quickest way down. When the snow softened I sat and slid the rest.

Loch Ossian was frozen but not very safe looking. We walked round rather than across. With skates it might have tempted us. How seriously we had taken our skating on The Moor those years ago. We were roped up, as for a climb, and had a loop attached to the rope (to stand in to crawl out if the ice collapsed) and even wore life jackets.

On another visit, walking along by Loch Ossian, we heard the frozen loch sizzling like an enormous frying pan of bacon on the go. Half the loch was water and a gale was smashing waves on to the frozen edge. This was breaking off flakes of ice which were then carried by the wind over the ice. The sound was caused by millions of sliding ice particles.

Charles's timing was perfect. The bothy brew was just ready when he came in out of the cold. It was cold, too, and I sat inside my sleeping bag until supper activity roused us. Weather permitting we planned to cross several hills to Rannoch Station the next day and catch the evening train back to Tulloch and motor on to a meet at Aviemore. It did not quite work out like that. The snow fell gently and steadily. We drank tea and chatted about The Moor. Charles had been very impressed by his winter view of it. "Most of Lakeland could be dropped into it."

I retold the story of our daft canoe crossing. It was a staff-pupil venture, and the Head came too. He chose a canoe at random and chose one that leaked—to the pupil's delight. The other teacher had canoed across the North Sea and at one stage said that was easier than Rannoch Moor which, believe it or not, was short of water. Rushing rivers were boulder fields. Loch Laidon at least gave several miles of water.

I was well ahead on Loch Laidon when my canoe grounded on a huge granite whaleback just below the surface. I jumped out, pulled the canoe over, and carried on. Later I heard the boys' impression. It appeared I suddenly stepped out of the canoe and began walking about on the water. Startled, one lad swore: "Christ!" only to have the quick retort, "Na, na, no Christ. Jist Hamish."

The Rannoch stationmaster was at a loss to know what to do with seven canoes. Did he measure them for length or did he weigh them? He chose the latter and we had a right old game taking a canoe in and out to the scales. It was the same blue canoe each time. It was the lightest. ("A gallon of water weighs 10lbs" and all that). If the stationmaster noticed he was too diplomatic to comment.

As Charles and I had not had to carry weight far on our backs we had fresh food for supper and good coffee to round it off. A multi-wheeled buggy swept up to the door and two keepers looked in for a bit. They'd seen the glow of our candles. "Just checking." Vandals and poachers even on Rannoch Moor! Charles headed for bed first and reported it was still snowing but there was no wind. "OK for tomorrow eh?" Half-an-hour later I went out—and met a blast of blowing snow. The tiger had turned.

All the tigers in the world seemed on the prowl that night and we lay listening to growls and groans and scrapes. Imagination made rather more of it than just a blizzard battering at an old, friendly howff.

When I thawed a hole in the window pane it was to look out on a world of driven snow. Drifts were deep behind any object and the trees were white down one side. We hurried to catch the morning train out.

The walk to the station was into the storm and we were glad of our modern Berghaus wind proofs. The dog thought it great fun and set off hunting grouse. He almost stood on one and nearly gave grouse, dog and humans heart-failure as it squawked into the air yelling at us to go-back, go-back, go-back. "Not bleeding likely," muttered Sheffield.

The grouse was the only dark object in a world of white. The dog turned white as well for the snow was driven into his outer coat where it clung to make a good insulation layer on top of his undercoat. His eyelashes even were snow-painted.

The stationmaster told us the train was hours late but once the plough went through it should follow. We had a four-hour wait: alternatively reading or making hot drinks when the cold penetrated too deeply. It was not a very violent storm but the drifts were over the platform and it looked impressive. A good day not to be on the hill—or The Moor.

The monster plough went through. It was right at the window

before we noticed it, by sight and feel rather than by sound. A goods struggled in and later the "up train" (normally the passenger trains pass each other at Tulloch) came in. Faces peered out with looks of wonder. We should have jumped in just for the run to Rannoch. That bit of line is as bleak as the Arctic. There is even a snow-tunnel at one place and the longest viaduct of the line leads to Rannoch Station.

I told Charles the story of the runaway train. A goods, heading north, somehow managed, by slowing down for the tablet and jerking off again, to detach its guard's van at Corrour. The guard was asleep at the time (the only stop was Crianlarich) and never noticed. The van ran back down the line.

At Rannoch it was spotted as it shot out the cutting on to the viaduct. Rules said it was to be derailed but that would be fatal for the guard. It was left alone and Gorton alerted. Gorton let it through and alerted Bridge of Orchy. He, too, let it through for the drag up to Auch would duly arrest the runaway. The stationmaster followed the train up and actually had to wake the guard who was quite unaware of his 25-mile solo journey across Rannoch Moor. On which cheery note Charles and I tumbled out for our brave Mallaig Express. The station family went, too, and the girls all gave the dog a cuddle. "What's his name?" There was a giggle when I told them: "Storm".

We reached Tulloch at noon and the radio said the A9 was blocked. There would be no meet. Perhaps we should stay west. If Rannoch Moor was blocked we could go round by Connell. It was, and we did. Charles admitted, "Ah well, the trip was worth it just to experience The Moor in those conditions". It was indeed.

Contrast is the jam in the layered cake of memory. This storm contrasted with remembered days of June heatwave when a gang of us crossed Rannoch Moor as part of a trek from Killin to Skye. Lying in the water all afternoon was our relief from the sun and next day we were up at 4 am to make it to Kingshouse before the midday sun could smite us again.

Where were you when President Kennedy was assassinated? It is one of those events which are so registered in memory that most people know where they were. I was in the middle of The Moor with another party, botanizing and exploring. We must have been some of the last people in the world to have heard the news. We were told about it three days after the event when some student friends joined us by train for the weekend. Until they produced *The Scotsman* we refused to believe them. It was just a nasty leg-pull.

Here is another man's Moor. See if you can recognise it.

"The mist rose and died away and showed us that country lying as waste as the sea; only the moorfowl and the peewits crying over it and far over to the east a herd of deer moving like dots. Much of it was red with heather; much of the rest broken up with bogs and hags and peaty pools; some had been burned black in a health fire; and in another place there was quite a forest of dead firs standing like skeletons. A wearier looking desert man never saw."

That was its first impression on Davie Balfour and Alan Breck Stewart in Stevenson's great yarn *Kidnapped*. It was not to be a tame Moor for them either. RLS obviously knew the place he described. Their journey would have to cross the Moor which had kidnapped its author.

Do you notice how we coin abbreviated titles for what we respect. Ben Nevis becomes simply The Ben and, when we say, briefly, The Moor, it can only be this fearsome, marvellous, romantic, untamable Moor of Rannoch.

8. Five Sisters of Kintail

THE Five Sisters of Kintail, The Three Sisters of Glen Coe. The National Trust, it seems, has a penchant for numerical mountains, or sisters in a row. The three Glen Coe summits are really just prows jutting out into the glen but the Sisters of Kintail are lined up in a tidy queue. They combine for one of the finest high-level walks in the country.

There are really far more than five peaks on the ridge but the most westerly five, seen so well over Loch Duich, have acquired this old nickname. The ridge runs along the whole of the north side of Glen Shiel, right to the Cluanie Inn, and the eastern half is well displayed to all who motor west along Loch Cluanie. Because I have spent several Hogmanay seasons in Kintail these peaks to me are magical winter mountains but they are big, brutal hills with little about them that can be termed sisterly.

The inexperienced walker will find them hard enough on a first summer visit but will not be content with one solitary visit. You cannot come to know Five Sisters in a day never mind the whole family of peaks guarding Glen Shiel to the north. There are plenty of surprises.

Sgurr Fhuaran is a goat peak—not in any translation of its name (which is not known for certain) but in a literal sense. The first time I was made aware of this was by nose rather than by sight.

I was wandering about on the seamed steepness above Glen Shiel in a thick mist when I became aware of a strong smell of animal. I crouched down and froze and in that breathy silence could hear the click-click of hooves on scree. Out of the mist hove a big billy goat, who stopped, nose quivering and big horns curved back over a damp-silvered neck.

In the mist he appeared huge as a mammoth. I don't think he saw me, though I was mere yards away, but some current of air must have taken my scent to him. He wheeled and clattered off into the murk.

Our mountain goats are not easy to see but Kintail is a place to walk with the sharper eyes of awareness. Often they were turned loose by shepherds in times gone by so they would occupy the craggy, dangerous slopes they like best—and so keep the silly sheep off. Their elusive descendants are there to this day.

Usually it is best to wander Scottish hills from west to east (with the prevailing weather) but I'd suggest the Five Sisters are traversed east-west so as to walk into the view of sunset and the islanded sea. There is another excellent reason: by starting up Glen Shiel you can save a thousand feet of severe slope-slogging. Sgurr Fhuaran is a big hill and you ascend all 1,068 metres of it. From the River Shiel to the summit is a horizontal distance of about two kilometres, so it could well be the longest and steepest gradient in the country. It certainly feels it.

That frontal assault is worth doing (once in a lifetime maybe) for it gives several interesting factors. You may meet the wild goats of Kintail (the four-legged ones that is), there is some setting and solving of route-finding problems, and the view out from this great wall of Kintail is superlative. There is also a unique chance to see the full range of mountain vegetation as height is gained. The tussocks and bogs, the myrtle-scented quakes, the alder-lined river lead to a curse of heather, so you feel like a flea trying to climb a hedgehog from tail to head. Escape to a scree gully and it is hung like a garden with purple saxifrage, butterwort and rose root.

When the heather fades with altitude, tormentil, thyme and other cheery flowers appear, then fade in turn. Moss campion, ladies alpine mantle, club mosses, and cowberry mark the nearing summit. It's as if every yard upwards was a degree northwards. On top of Scotland you are touching Arctic tundra.

The bird life goes through this change, too. By the River Shiel there will be the cheery flitting and bobbing of the hyperactive dipper and wagtail. In the heather you will be scolded by wren and grated at by stonechat. On the tops you may meet ptarmigan and raven, or hear the lovely voices of mountain blackbird or golden plover. Eagles soar high above these ragged ridges. This varied, familiar, but never less than thrilling, range of wildlife is one of the least-acknowledged but most influential reason why walkers stray up mountains. You experience several worlds (and probably several climates) whenever you climb a hill.

The Kintail hills enjoy unrestricted access at all times and it is a good plan to save walks on them (or Torridon, Glen Coe and other mountain properties of the Trust) for the stalking season (mid-August to mid-October usually) in order not to spoil other peoples'

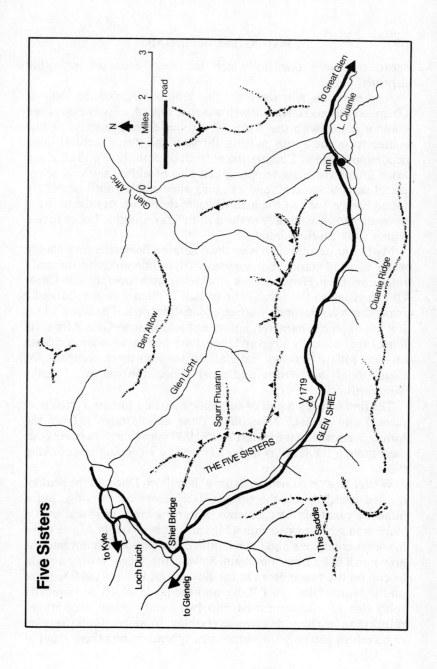

Five Sisters

N

0 1 2 3
Miles

road

to Kyle

Loch Duich

Shiel Bridge

to Glenelg

The Saddle

THE FIVE SISTERS

GLEN SHIEL

X 1719

Sgurr Fhuaran

Glen Licht

Ben Attow

Glen Affric

Inn

L. Cluanie

Cluanie Ridge

to Great Glen

sport, especially one on which the local economy probably depends.

As well as the hills there are fine long passes and the Falls of Glomach too make Kintail well worth a visit. Access is easy, even without a car, with the Kyle railway line from Inverness or bus routes from the south passing through the glen. There is hotel accommodation at Cluanie and at the foot of the glen and all along Loch Duich there are tempting bed and breakfast signs. A shop, petrol station, caravan and camping sites and a youth hostel are found by the head of the loch. Despite these facilities the hills are never crowded, especially in the non-holiday months. Let us take a winter walk on the summits.

My favourite approach is up the Caorainn Beag stream: a cheery water of vivid clarity that somehow tricks one up on to the main ridge unnoticed. Here there is a tiny lochan on a triple col with Ciste-Dhubh rising to the north. The lochan is often frozen solid and I remember a school party once enjoying slides on it. The Black Chest is a hill of some character, jutting out into remote Glen Affric. Its flanks are unusually steep and there have been avalanche accidents on them following heavy snowfalls. After a northern excursion for Ciste-Dhubh we return and work along the queue of peaks westwards.

The first is really a pair of summits: Sgurr an Fhuarail ("the cold place") and Aonach Mheadhoin ("the middle ridge"). Only the former is named on the walker's 1:50,000 map (Sheet 33 covers our day) though the latter is higher. There is a swooping crest linking them.

Wester Ross is gained on Sgurr a' Bhealaich Dheirg, "the peak of the red pass," where the summit itself is not on the ridge but a hundred yards out along a spur, a narrow crest, crowded with a stone wall and crowned with a big cairn. It is an oddly Alpine extra in winter conditions and from it little Ciste-Dhubh juts out into the grey north like a huge mountain. Saileag, the "heel," is only a slight hiccup on the sweep down to the Bealach an Lapain, the low point on the North Glen Shiel Ridge and the place which conveniently splits this 15 kilometre crest into two more normal expeditions, rather than one huge day over everything. In winter this is the point of no return and only the virtuous early-starters and those stout of

The Five Sisters of Kintail

limb will have daylight enough to continue for the Five Sisters proper.

Sgurr na Spainteach is the peak of the Spaniard, this improbable name recalling the least-known of Jacobite risings in 1719, when 300 unfortunate Iberians landed in Kintail and were captured on the slopes of this hill.

The battle site is just above the Telford Bridge which is well seen from where the improved road swings across from one side of the glen to the other.

A storm had scattered the invaders' fleet but this band and several notable Jacobites (including the Keiths, later to become famous European generals) did land, only to be trapped by Government warships which pounded Eileann Donan Castle. Rob Roy Macgregor joined the small army as it set off up Glen Shiel but they ran into the Scottish C.I.C., General Wightman, and were eventually scattered.

Flanking the ridge past Sgurr na Spainteach is a strange fissure as if the hill were splitting open. You see this in the grey Corries and other hills too. Under snow conditions you have simulated crevasses and I've seen a happy walker suddenly drop out of sight on two occasions, a rather alarming experience. From Sgurr na Ciste Duibhe (another one) there is quite a drop to a col and on up Sgurr na Carnach (hill of stones), then a small drop and the final pared cone of Sgurr Fhuaran.

The corries on the right are deeply cut and cliff-edged with the schisty slabs set at steep angles. Sgurr nan Saighead, the next (triple-headed) Sister, is "peak of the arrows"—and the strata looks like bundles of arrows. The last Sister, Sgurr na Moraich, is the "peak of the sea flats," and it dominates the low-flying meadows and tidal acres where the Croe enters Loch Duich. It is a pity we can't translate Sgurr Fhuaran; however, as senior sister, she is well able to look after herself. As a viewpoint Sgurr Fhuaran is one of the finest in Britain.

A traveller passing down Glen Shiel in 1803 wrote of the slope above him as being "an inclined wall, of such inaccessible height that no living creature would venture to scale it." Attitudes change and thanks to the generosity of one mountaineer, Percy Unna, these mountains were bought for the National Trust of Scotland—and plenty of living creatures (this goat included) have ventured to scale them, adding them to our treasured "far golden hills of memory."

9. *Skye Alternatives*

THE Black Cuillin is such a mesmeric range of mountains that once visitors have reached Glenbrittle it is very hard for them to wander anywhere else in Skye. It took several years before I realised that one of the secrets of success in Skye was mobility. It was midges that drove the point home under the thick skin of my preconditioning.

On those warm, balmy, summer days, when campers sat wearing gloves and balaclavas to cook supper, the midges could become intolerable. As soon as the wind from the west vanished they seemed to call up a task force and launch an all out attack. We would flee: to Broadford or Uig Youth Hostels, or to repitch our tents at Sligachan if the wind had just changed to easterly. We became experts at that game: east wind, camp at Sligachan and walk and climb from there; west wind, camp in Glenbrittle and operate on that side.

This led to noticing how, even in a compact range like the Black Cuillin, there could be several weathers influencing the hills. Glenbrittle peaks could be clouded and wet while the Gillean end was dappled with sun and shadow; sharp, clear and dry. It also led us to go up the Red Cuillin as well as the Black, to traverse the viewpoint hills on the "wrong" side of Glenbrittle, to wander the coast—all below the level of the dirty tricks being played on the summits of the big hills.

Skye is actually as much a walkers' paradise as a climbers' Valhalla yet, while the latter flock to the island like urban starlings, the former seem only to flit through as stray migrants. Perhaps the fame of the Black Cuillin as the climbers' kingdom has a discouraging effect on walkers. Skye is for the rock apes and not the bunnies. Nothing could be further from the truth and even the fortress of the Black Cuillin is a fake. There is plenty of rewarding walking in its hills.

It is strange how wrong impressions can become ingrained. If you mention Loch Coruisk to most people they at once see a black hole, surrounded by cliffs, where the sun never penetrates. It was just such a picture that was painted by artists as notable as Turner or written about with poetic licence by Sir Walter Scott. Their romantic inspirations linger on still. It is the popular image of Coruisk.

71

Loch Coruisk in fact faces south, the hills are set well back, it is a suntrap, relished by an abundant flora and birdlife. It even has a convenient climbing hut yet, for every bednight there, the hut in Glenbrittle will ring up a hundred though for romantic setting Coruisk is unbeatable. "It always rains at Coruisk" has done its work. It rains no more at Coruisk than at the Glenbrittle. It can rain with considerable determination at both when it sets its mind to it.

Years ago, in the Sligachan Hotel, I heard a lovely aside between two solemn-faced locals who were filling in a wet October evening in the bar. "Aye Donald, it has been raining since June now," the first man said. The other considered for a minute, blew out a puff of smoke, then asked, "Just so. Just so. *Which* June?"

Skye is so called because the sky is always falling on it! The weather cracks about Skye are legion. "Have you been on Skye this summer?" a lady asked a friend in Kyle. "No dear, I was in Inverness that day." There is certainly a hint of meteorological instability about Skye, which is why this business of "playing it" is important. I have had many unbearable heatwave spells as well as some memorable washouts.

On one September school party we endured several days of rain, gales, hail and sleet on the Glenbrittle campsite before we fled. We applied our mobility practice to an extreme; one lad later wrote in the school magazine, "We had a most successful expedition to Skye. We climbed every Munro in the Cairngorms."

It does not always need quite such drastic mobility to make the best of a bad Cuillin. Let me describe one day I had last year which, to me, is as much Skye magic as a climb on Sron na Ciche or traversing another section of Ridge or climbing one of the Munros. Having mentioned Munros let me make a plea to Munro-baggers to work away at Skye *soon* rather than late in their careers. I know several delightful old folk who "have done all the Munros except one or two in Skye."

Sir Hugh Munro himself never did get up the Inaccessible Pinnacle, all that stood between him and a champagne party on the late, lamented, Carn Cloich Mhuilinn. By walking standards these are challenging Munros, with some scrambling, much exposure and in a few cases, serious, though technically easy, climbing. There are

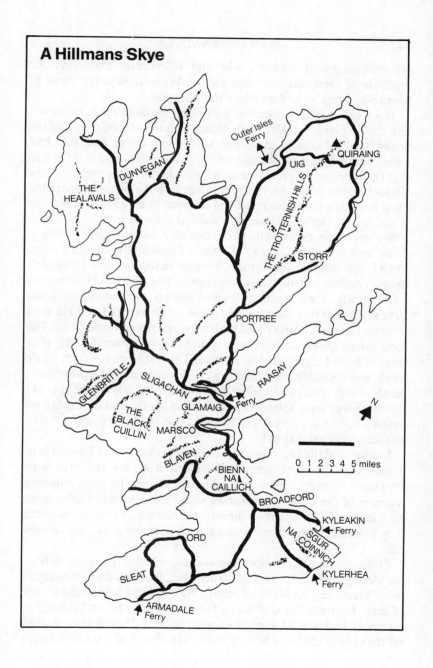

A Hillmans Skye

Outer Isles Ferry

QUIRAING

DUNVEGAN

UIG

THE HEALAVALS

THE TROTTERNISH HILLS

STORR

PORTREE

RAASAY

GLENBRITTLE

SLIGACHAN

Ferry

GLAMAIG

THE BLACK CUILLIN

MARSCO

BLAVEN

BIENN NA CAILLICH

BROADFORD

N

0 1 2 3 4 5 miles

KYLEAKIN
← Ferry

SGUR NA COINNICH

ORD

KYLERHEA
← Ferry

SLEAT

ARMADALE
↑ Ferry

scrambling guidebooks to help and Glenbrittle maintains the tradition of professional Cuillin guides. Without Skye the game of Munro-bagging would be much the poorer.

The Cuillin on this occasion was being made difficult because I had the dog with me. The week before he had romped over half the peaks on the Ridge as there was good snow cover. But, that had gone in days of rain which had turned to snow showers and frost as night so there was a great deal of *verglas* on the rocks and the snow slopes became iron hard, fine for crampons but a bit too demanding for a dog. The tops also remained covered in cloud, day after day while, below, the sun shone. We walked elsewhere.

We drove up Glenbrittle early one day and wiggled over and down and round and up to the main Sligachan-Dunvegan road. Skye is full of unvisited corners because reaching them gives such devious driving, often on dead-end roads. The A863 to Dunvegan is a fast, newish road. It climbs high so there is a grand view of Loch Bracadale with its scattering of islands, while across Loch Harport the lego-like croft houses lined high above prows of vertical cliff. The road swept down and across a causeway and immediately after there is a road signposted to Portree. This is the moor road, single track, and about the only road in Skye where you can forget you are on an island. You can be all of four miles from salt water! It is my favourite way from Glenbrittle to Portree. At the end of the day we dashed across it to visit the bakery, one of the regular wet-day attractions of the capital.

Just beyond the causeway there is a plain church and I pulled in to it and went into the graveyard behind it to see the graves of Professor Norman Collie and John Mackenzie, the great climbing pioneers of the Cuillin. Mackenzie was a local lad and Collie spent his last years in Skye, cut off there by the last war, so it is appropriate they lie beside each other, having shared so many great days on the hill.

Collie is one the most interesting of the pioneers whose wanderings took him to the Caucauses, Rockies and Himalayas (with Mummery on Nanga Parbat). He was busy behind the scenes of early Everest attempts' was a famous scientist (neon lighting for instance), had one of the greatest collections of Chinese jade, started off the saga of the Grey Man of Beinn Macdhui and even took an ice

Hamish and Storm, a view to the Black Cuillin from the western hills above Glenbrittle

axe to cut a hold on Lakeland rock. Of all the pioneers he is the one I would most like to have known. (A biography of Collie, by Christine Mill should be out soon so keep an eye open for it.)

You cannot hurry travel in Skye. A mile on, through the village of Struan, I stopped to visit the broch of Dun Beag. This is the best-preserved in the island and is being made into a showpiece. A team was working on it and we swopped yarns about brochs in Shetland and chambered cairns in Caithness which they had worked on. What a satisfying job I thought: outdoors, restoring fascinating prehistoric sites, in beautiful surroundings. From their cheery chat they obviously had good job satisfaction. They sent me down to see a *souterrain* on the other side of the roads, one of those strange mystery structures, long, stone-built "rooms" set underground for uses long-forgotten.

I resisted going into Dunvegan then and turned west towards the Macleod's Tables: Healaval Mhor (469m) and Healaval Beag (489m). These are flat-topped, steeply-sloped hills that are prominent shapes from all over the island. There is also a smaller one nearer Idrigill Point—Macleod's Coffee Table perhaps? Did you notice that *Mhor*, meaning *big*, is lower than *Beag,* meaning *small*?

As with Aonach Mor and Beag next to Ben Nevis the name applies to bulk rather than height. The flatness gave rise to an incident several hundred years ago when the weather was either different or Macleod had a hot line to the devil who controls such things.

The then chief had been summoned to court along with many others. At a state banquet a mainland earl taunted Macleod with such comments as "You never saw a table this size in the islands ... Have you such a hall in all the west? ... Did you ever see such candles?" (pointing at the chandeliers that lit the impressive occasion). Eventually the Macleod could take no more and challenged his tormentor to visit Dunvegan where he promised he would find a table larger and a hall finer and a feast better lit than any place in Edinburgh could provide.

A year later many of the original company gathered at Dunvegan. They were led up a new path to the summit of Healaval Bheag, Macleod's Table, where a feast was spread and the starry night was brightened by a circle of clansmen holding flaming

Summer peacefulness—Portree, the "capital" of Skye

torches. "Here is my table, gentlemen. Though the smaller of my two, has the king a larger one? Here are my candlesticks: faithful followers worth more than gold. Here is my hall, with God's Heaven for roof. Who could have finer?" He won his wager but I'd like to know how he fixed the weather.

I parked off a side road. A knoll above, ringed with crag, was marked as a prehistoric fort and from a distance its square of green, in a sea of brown moor, was a useful landmark. We followed up a slot of burn where a couple of peregrines were chattering away.

Storm put up a snipe and from the first rise where we could look across Glen Osdale to Healaval Mhor I was aware of a buzzard mewing overhead while both curlews and golden plovers, with their plaintive cries, were drowning out the skylarks' irrepressible song. You don't have that vibrant life on the barren heights of the Black Cuillin.

The ridge rose gradually over a couple of miles to end at a dark upsurge of crag. We had a rest under the crag after toiling up the grassed-over skirts of scree. A small boulder fell and went skittering down the slope. Storm obviously thought it was some new form of wildlife and went pell-mell after it. When it stopped he was very puzzled. I rolled a few more down and he soon learned this was a cheat; my smell was on these very dead objects. That game stopped when we noticed another figure coming up. We skirted round and up the crag to a saddle, beyond which a short rise led to the edge of Macleod's Table. The sun came out so I quickly dug out the cameras and lay in wait for a foreground figure.

Loch Bracadale seemed as full of islands as Clew Bay from Croag Patrick. It was a scene of silver tones which ranged from shining sea waters to almost black over the cloud-capped Cuillin, whose northern corries still held plenty of snow. Away to the east the apparent whale-back ridges of Trotternish were also dusted white. I knew this was only half the truth for, out of sight, on the east side lay miles of cliffs and corries and spectacular rock formations. Were there no Black Cuillin people would still stand in awe by The Old Man of Storr or the haunting weirdness of the Quiraing. The Cuillin of Rhum were hove-to on one far horizon and away in the west the peaks of Harris broke through the haze of another.

I was so busy looking at the view I almost missed my photograph of the walker on the crest of the ridge. We continued over the plateau to the trig point together. A cold wind made it too uncomfy to linger. I set off down and along the terraced flank of an intervening hill to find a lunch spot out of the wind. Healaval Mhor loomed above, a tawny lion (*couchant*) but edged in white where the plateau edge had caught the snow. The other walker passed with a greeting and set off through the bogs of the col. An old trick I sometimes played on our school gangs suddenly galvanised me into action, proving just the spur to force lazy legs into using their muscles.

The curve of this larger Table mountain was quite marked on the slope above the col and if Storm and I could gain the slope 200 yards along we'd be able to climb out of sight. We set off in pursuit and as we left the col were only 50 yards apart, but people are usually watching their footing on rough ground and we kept on to vanish round the hillside. I kept going round and brutally upwards, pleased to see lungs took it even if calf muscles protested vigorously at the unaccustomed exercise. We reached the plateau. It was empty, except for the large cairn and we were lying in its lee looking very lazy when the walker arrived. "How did you get here?" his looks cried.

The top of this northern Table is so wide that you can see little surrounding landscape from the summit, just the top of Healaval Bheag in fact. It would be a good place for annual dinners of the Flat Earth Society. Storm and I walked to the edge of the world and fell off—at least it felt like that. We descended steeply to Glen Osdale that drains this horseshoe of hills so as to angle along back to the car. The *dun* knoll above the car simplified navigation. We aimed for its green square. By the river we had a brew and gladly would have lingered on what could have been a delectable camp site.

Down the glen we looked across to Dunvegan Castle and the town scattered along the head of the loch, yet where we lay felt utterly peaceful and remote. The perpetual lark song, the fall of water and the wind in the heather were the only sounds—till a jet fighter screamed past below us and set his trailing din echoing round the corries.

Dunvegan Castle, Skye's major wet-weather attraction, after Portree's bakery, we knew well so we quickly drove over to Glendale and Neist Point lighthouse which nestles among thousand-foot cliffs, the highest in Skye and the island's furthest west. The landscape took on a stark, simplified cubist form, the dark Cuillin clouds had spread and the air was heavy with approaching storm. Glendale needs a day to explore both its scenery and its sites, it needs a second day to walk the coastal path round by the sea stacks of Macleod's Maidens, and a third, of course, to climb the Macleod's Tables. One out of three was not even a pass mark for the Duirinish Peninsula but the day had been blessed by cool winds, kindly sun, good walking surfaces and the sort of panoramic views only islands can give. There is always next time. God willing.

We returned to Glenbrittle and as we stepped out of the car the rain began; but we were content, knowing that Glenbrittle, even with its hills covered in cloud, is not a tragedy. It is an opportunity to explore an alternative Skye.

10. The Empty Quarter

TO set off into the wilderness south of An Teallach, several hours before dawn, at the winter equinox, is not uncommon. It is big country and to do anything worth while hours have to be borrowed from the stars, morning and evening. However, to set off in shirt sleeves as on this last occasion was ridiculous.

I had carried in a heavy pack the day before, across the moors, in Bogtrotters rather than boots, and the ground only stopped being saturated on the ridges of An Teallach itself. Strath ne Sealga was orange-tinted with the westering sun as we descended to the bothy. Tom Weir in his ever-fresh book of youthful doings "Highland Days" tells of staying with a family in the house just before the war. It has been deserted since, but kept weatherproof as a gangrels' haven.

Storm and I settled in the back room, with a table against the west window to catch the last squint of light, a bench to sit on and our bedding rolled out along one side. I'd brought in some meat and fresh vegetables and a poke of prepared spices—so relished a warming curry. (I'd thought that a good idea for the depths of the winter). Sleep was poor, with the dog diving after mice periodically, and I was far too warm in the heavy sleeping bag. You don't expect the weather to be curried a few days before Christmas.

The alarm went off at five and we were away an hour later with meusli, scrambled eggs and many cups of tea inside. I'd carried in my boots to keep them dry for wearing above the freezing level but as this was probably about 10,000 feet I kept to the wee-wellies, my well-used Bogtrotters. Their light weight I'm sure is the equivalent of an extra three miles in a day's walk. In this landscape of Christmas pudding and custard, dry feet is the real treat.

So warm had the night been that the river had risen several inches and the spot I'd found to cross was now just over, rather than under the top of my Bogtrotters. We had to paddle. Melting remnants of snow ensured the water was not warm! There was a big moon and the torch was hardly needed for the boggy flounder across to the next river. Snipe shot off with modest compaint. The dog dived on a mouse and killed it, probably in frustration at his unsuccessful night's efforts. The second crossing took longer and toes tingled painfully afterwards. The first mile had taken an hour.

It had landed us, however, on a good "made" path which leads through to the Fionn Loch and on to Poolewe eventually, and we could stomp on with some rhythm in our steps. Beinn Dearg Mor (which has a high corrie like a mouthful of fangs) loomed over us and so hid the moon that the torch had to be used. When Junction Buttress loomed out of the night we swung right up a side valley. It is a short glen and at the top of it a 1,000 foot waterslide rushes down what seems a dead end.

A grudging daylight girned out from the murk but nothing can detract from the magic mile. The dead-end of the glen has been craftily scaled by secret zigzags and from the lip above the view explodes. North, over a turquoise-grey loch, was the sliced-off cone of Beinn Dearg Beag and the forgotten corrie of Beinn Dearg Mor, down the valley, in true bird's eye view (an eagle's eye surely), the glen was suddenly moving with stags while, beyond, An Teallach, a great among greats, sent plumes of cloud across the fading stars. This is one of those great "doorway" spots of nature. You marvel at this view behind—and marvel at the sweep ahead.

Between here and Loch Maree is the wildest, roughest, rock-and-water country in Britain. It beggars description. It also excludes all but the hardiest walkers or far-gone Munro-baggers for its miles are stretched and its hours shortened. After three hours of walking hard I was only just below my first desired summit—and I'd started in the wilderness, not the more-distant road. No peak in the Lake District is *three* miles from a road, never mind five hours walking from the tarmac. The scale, as ever, was brutally apparent.

A path off the path twisted up by the Big Cold Loch (Fuar Loch Mor) and under the red bluff of Ruadh Stac Mor, one of those newish Munros which came in with the OS re-surveying the area. I left my rucker below it, at a boulder howff, and wandered up, still in shirt sleeves. It was the only summit I was to have clear. It was a new Munro for the dog Storm; this raid being made for his sake—that being my defence as to why I was there yet again—as if you needed a reason for straying south from Loch Broom!

Ruadh Stac Mor had a special Munro place in my affections for on it I had completed a "solo" round of these listed summits, something which had taken many years for the remoter or harder the peaks the more they seemed to have attracted companions. ("I

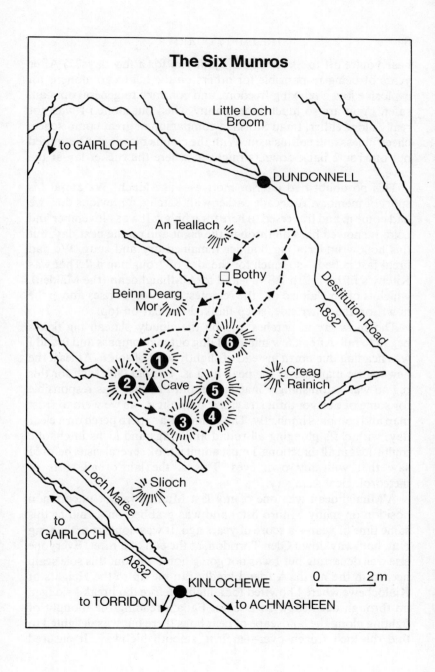

The Six Munros

Little Loch Broom

to GAIRLOCH

DUNDONNELL

An Teallach

Bothy

Beinn Dearg Mor

Destitution Road

A832

1

6

2

Cave

5

Creag Rainich

3

4

Slioch

Loch Maree

to GAIRLOCH

A832

0   2 m

KINLOCHEWE

to TORRIDON

to ACHNASHEEN

hear you're off to Skye. Could I join you for a few days?") After years of being responsible for others on the hill to go alone is an explosive joy, a relaxing freedom, and contrary to general opinion, safer. (You are so much more canny when out alone.) I was not really alone either, I had Storm, a companion of great competence, cheerfulness and enthusiasm. With the clouds blowing in he sniffed out our route back down, straight to where the rucker lay at the cave.

This no doubt had ulterior motives—like lunch! We ate at his sport of memory. A decade earlier with Kitchy, a previous dog, we had come in and traversed to here for a bivvy. It was November and cold. It snowed hard all through the night and on the next day, but this hollow under a big boulder remained dry and snug. We had breakfast in bed—so much for the idea of "roughing it." That was Kitchy's fifth visit to RSM—and to A'Mhaighdean (the Maiden), which is often claimed as "the remotest Munro." It rises above the howff on the other side, steep-flanked but flat on top.

The snow lay in patches and on the cloudy plateau big flakes began to fall. After a few minutes I dug out my compass and found I was heading due north instead of slightly west of south. At least the new metric map shows the peak as it is. The old One Inch for this region was astonishingly inaccurate and I'm sure was responsible for some of our youthful strayings, brought up as we were to trust map and compass implicitly. The summit is a superb perch on a clear day, with cliffs plunging all round and crags and lochs in chaotic multitudes in all directions. I must admit it took several visits before I saw that with my own eyes. This is the lair of all sorts of meteorological savagery.

A'Mhaighdean was one of my last Munros (a not uncommon position on many Munro lists) and was grabbed on a raid at this same time of year—a score of years ago. It was done from the Ling Hut, half-way down Glen Torridon, at the end of a meet. Everyone else was departing but I was not going home without this sole scalp needed in the north. A friend kindly ran me up to the Heights of Kinlochewe where I howffed for a night. Before daybreak I slogged up through deep snow to Lochan Fada, dreading the thought of fighting along the landscape of peat bogs there but was delighted to find the loch frozen over—a firm, smooth highway. It ensured

Storm with An Teallach beyond; on the expedition round the "Big Six"

success but even so I ran out of daylight and had a long tramp back to, and down, Glen Torridon. I was quite pleased to see, 20 years on, I was still prepared to tackle the Maiden in December with the assurance of a night return to base.

We took a bearing off the summit down to the boggy col and Beinn Tarsuinn beyond. It is a deep pass and there was no escape from the tops for many miles beyond. We were truly committed and as so often happens under these circumstances, the body seemed to respond. Our pace increased and the lethargy of recovering from a cold seemed to vanish.

Beinn Tarsuinn felt a winter peak: a bastion of ice-rimmed sandstone set against the wild north. We scuttled along like timid sentries on its ramparts, and descended the stepped stratas beyond. Tarsuinn means *across* and every hill so named is very much one linking mightier things on either side, to be traversed (not skirted) with some respect. This Tarsuinn occupied a special place in the Munro's Tables I grew up with for then there were "276 Munros, with Beinn Tarsuinn, 277." We, naturally, made it 277.

The One Inch map showed Tarsuinn about 400 feet below the magical height but Victorian hillgoers with their barometers had long ago noted it was above the magic altitude. Hence the laconic footnote in the Tables. Hence why the new maps are vitally important to safety and accurate navigation in places like this or north of Glen Affric where the original mapping was so extraordinarily inaccurate.

A convenient trace of path skirts a small craggy peak that stands in the way. This day it was clearly shown up by a dusting of snow. It led to the foot of Mullach Coire Mhic Fhearchair, the day's main peak and the only one over the big, if unromantic 1,000 metres.

The Mullach had a genuine winter feel to it and a blowing mist on top had us quickly setting the compass and roaming on down. Summits are not always the best place for lingering. Puffing up Sgurr Ban I realised time was running out—and I really *was* feeling weak from the effects of my cold. The dog would quite happily have gone on for ever. (He is the Munro-bagger of the family). The first bumslide of the season (a wet 300ft) helped us down to the col beyond Sgurr Ban. We shared a piece by the loch and enjoyed the rest. A shower sweeping up the glen arched a rainbow over Beinn

Dearg Mor. It had been a good day. We chuntered down into dusk.

There, at valley level again, the worst of the day was to come. The ground was a chaotic, messy wetness, full of bogs and rotting tree stumps, of humps and hollows and ambushing streams.

At least the river edge had grassy banks but we followed them too far and cutting across to the river below the bothy we ran into several meandering streams: peat-black, waist-deep—and just too wide to jump. The last river let us off lightly and I crossed without removing my Bogtrotters. A glow from the bothy window indicated company for the evening. The back straightens. One enters ever so casually.

"Hi."

"Hi."

"Had a good day?"

"Aye, great, just great."

11. *Handa Island*

"**H**ANDA. Where's that?"

Such was the reaction of most people when they heard I was off to this island. A few climbing and ornithologist friends knew enough to mutter "The Great Stack of Handa" but not much more. It is an elusive spot.

Handa (Sandy Isle) lies about 20 minutes south of Cape Wrath as the gull flies, off that northern, scoured, watered landscape of grey rock with Loch Laxford to the north and Scourie round a headland to the south. Further south the land runs out along the horizon to end, with a flourish, at the slender pinnacle of the Old Man of Stoer. West, over sea, lie the sunset lands terminating at the Butt of Lewis.

Fiona Beveridge (a biology student from Edinburgh) and I had let ourselves in for a stint of voluntary wardening. The island is a bird sanctuary (thanks to the efforts of the late George Waterston) run by the RSPB and is manned from April to mid-September. The last month was ours, seeing out the dandelion days of a delectable summer.

To reach Handa, Fiona had to travel by bus, train, train, bus, postbus and ferry, bringing with her all she needed for coping with the west's erratic weather, plus food for a week. I had been wandering in Sutherland, and after a birthday climb of Ben Stack drove to the ferry at Tarbert where Robert MacLeod, one of the hamlet's crofter-fisherman took me the mile and a quarter across to land on the sands of Traigh an Teampaill.

The beach exists, one of several arcs of white shell sand backed by dunes and machair, but there was no sign of a chapel. On a bit, though, the machair was studded with stones and one larger (early nineteenth-century) grave slab with *Peter Morrison* on it. This was one of those island burial sites favoured in the days when wolves still roamed Scotland and were apt to disturb the dead.

Beside this spot, built on the site of an old fishermen's bothy there is a day shelter for visitors with displays and information about the island wildlife. Handa does not go in for rarities so visitors tend to be curious tourists, or genuine bird enthusiasts, with the species-listing "twitcher" happily absent. One of us would usually welcome any

The Great Stack of Handa in Sutherland

boatful of visitors and give them a map of the circular walk that has been laid out. This takes up to three hours to go round.

Visitors are asked to keep to a marked route, partly because the centre is featureless and they can become disorientated easily, but mainly to protect nesting birds. If eggs, or young, are left exposed at all the robber skuas are there in a flash. Unlike many marked "nature trails" this circuit loses nothing in wildlife or scenic interest by being a made path followed by all. The queachy ground discourages straying.

The skuas are one of the more unusual birds (with the attributes of stukas) and there are both great and arctic skuas breeding. They accept people on the path and so can easily be seen, but if anyone strays they will be vigorously attacked. The sound of the querulous arctics is one of the background sounds to life in the wardens' bothy.

This is a one-time shepherd's cottage lying up behind fank and walled "park," where the desert and the sown once met. It has a wind-seared stand of lodgepole pine beside it, this shelter belt protecting a planting of native trees: alder, birch, willows, rowan, sallow, hazel and holly. I brought out two dozen birch as there were very few of this commoner local species. Crofters still run sheep on the island, but the numbers have dropped over the years and the vegetation is winning back the quality lost in the familiar past of overgrazing and burning. Handa, is some ways, is a microcosm of Sutherland history.

James Wilson in his book *A Voyage Round the Coasts of Scotland* (1842) found the island tenanted by 12 families "who though forming a loyal people, have curiously enough combined to establish a queen of their own in the person of the oldest widow." Subsistence, he noted, was partly fishing, sea-fowl and eggs. They also exported feathers. This was in 1841. The numbers of families dropped to seven and the potato famines of mid-century was a final catastrophe leading to the people being cleared to America. They were native Gaelic speakers but no doubt their marching orders came in Queen's English.

In 1848 the "sportsman" Charles St John (who contributed so much to the clearing of birds, including Sutherland's last Osprey) visited Handa, not long after the evacuation, and described their

A fulmar chick on Handa Island—able to spit oil a good few yards even at this age!

croft houses lying desolate and overrun by starlings. On the rocks a large white cat sat "looking wistfully towards the mainland." One of the boatmen commented, "She is wanting the ferry."

Mammals are scarce; apart from the plentiful rabbits, there being only a few brown rats (mainly shore-living), pygmy shrews—and otters. Grey seals come in to the flat skerries (the bases of long-fallen sea stacks) and various whales, porpoises and dolphins swept in and out of the view of binoculars while we were there, something to make up for the auks having flown off to their mystery winter grounds.

Harvie-Brown provides some interesting information in his books at the turn of the century and quite a succession of well-known authors have mentioned the islands: Ratcliffe Barnett, Seton Gordon, Robert Atkinson ("Island Going"), Alasdair Alpin MacGregor ("Islands by the Score"), Campbell Steven ("The Island Hills". Handa only makes 406 feet, but the island slopes steadily upwards from the south to end in sheer cliffs only slightly lower than that: a magnificent bastion battered by the attacking Minch. The sandstone is broken into fissures and caves, stacks and skerries and its strata ensures plenty of ledge room for the 100,000 guillemots, razorbills, fulmars, puffins, shags, kittiwakes and other birds.

Climbers have a more specialised interest in Handa's Great Stack and this apparently impregnable rock tower has had men on top of it on three or four occasions.

Harvie-Brown, writing of the 1870s says it was reached by a Uist party, called in at the laird's behest to clear off the summit-nesting black-backed gulls. They were supposed to have thrown a line across the 80 foot gap and caught hold, somehow, and a boy sent over with a strong rope. It sounds a bit dubious and may be a garbled version of a well-authenticated visit about that time by a party from Lewis.

Their objective was to cull the birds and they were skilled fowlers with regular experience of the cliffs of Sula Sgeir and North Rona. The history of climbing always ignores this early use of ropes and climbing techniques. The Great Stack was tackled as a fun-challenge rather than for any urgency in collecting food. It was an escapade of quite remarkable boldness, carried out simply and effectively.

The route from sea-level had been looked at but the bird-slimy ledges and initial overhangs discouraged the ascent. Ninety years later Tom Patey found this equally true and both his and the Lewis parties reached the Stacks summit—horizontally.

The Great Stack stands in the mouth of a deep-cut *geo* (creek) so they took the ends of a 600ft rope out the opposite arms until the centre of the rope was trailing across the green summit plateau of the stack. The ends were secured thoroughly and a renowned fowler-climber, Donald MacDonald, set off to cat-crawl along the rope: 400ft above the smashing waves in a bedlam of frightened birds with no security at all. MacDonald had some difficulty on gaining the edge (due to the sag of the rope) but desperation gave an extra surge to land him, gasping, on the top.

Stakes were hauled over and the rope firmly anchored on the stack before a bo'sun's chair was rigged and the culling of the birds began. The stakes remained visible till after Hitler's war, a startling, improbable testimony to the feat.

On the first of July 1967, Dr Tom Patey, with Chris Bonington and Ian MacNaught-Davis, arrived to repeat the Lewis-mens route to the summit. Even with all the aids of modern climbing it was a slow, difficult crossing and Tom alone made the journey. The nylon rope stretched and sagged as soon as Tom's weight came on to it. Jumar clamps, gadgets for sliding up vertical ropes (and giving one holds as they grip when weight comes on them), do not work so well when used at angles approaching the horizontal. It took three quarters of an hour of exhausting struggle to cross. Birds crashed into the ropes and Tom noticed, while dangling in the middle, that a guillemot was "pecking thoughtfully at the taut rope" where it crossed its territory.

A few days later this team were busy with the televised ascent of the Old Man of Hoy. One of the team was Hamish MacInnes, and on the first of August 1969 (with the Stack clearer of birds) he, G.N. Hunter and D.F. Lang finally climbed the Great Stack of Handa from sea-level. The latter two also climbed the smaller stack in Puffin Bay.

Tom Patey was tragically killed when abseiling off another Sutherland sea stack in Loch Eriboll in 1971.

One evening the permanent summer warden, Mike Walker, came

rushing up to find Fiona and me to say that Robert the boatman would take us by sea to the Great Stack. We grabbed pullovers and cameras and scampered to the shore.

There are several other, lesser, stacks, a huge curtain-wall of north-facing cliff and my eye of imagination was busy tracing possible climbing routes, a perfectly safe speculation, being past all possibility of actually doing anything. If only it had been 20 years ago.

The Great Stack bulked large over us, the whitewashed ledges empty and silent, a monolithic silence to which was added a sudden gloom as Robert swung the boat in to go round the stack itself. The passage barely left room for the startled shags to dive between boat and vertical cliffs. The walls were riddled with caves and passages. The Great Stack stands on a very rotten base.

Handa, for me, was a marvellous return to nature, to a way of life ruled by weather rather than worksheets. It was hard work but to a purpose. You saw the results. And you could lift eyes to the hills at any time. There were always the sounds of sanity: divers flying overhead, the cat-crying arctic skuas, running water, the chug-chug of an outboard, the heart-beat of the sea, the impatient wind winding over the island.

John Ridgway visited the island several times while we were there (his Ardmore Outdoor Centre is just up the coast) Fiona and I waved to *English Rose IV* as he and Andy Briggs set off on their round the world non-stop trip. That remarkable feat, which knocked about two months of the record, is told in their book "Round the World Non-Stop"

A sad and ironic footnote though was the news, from John, that Robert, the canny boatman, had been drowned in Handa Sound, while they, sticking their necks out for months on end, had returned home to the north hale and hearty.

BIG TREKS

*From what has gone before it is obvious that one of my
joys is big treks within these small islands of our.
Circumstances seldom allow most people more than a
couple of weeks so the following is a clutch of tales of
trans-Scotland hikes—something possible for anyone.
How about you?*

12. Ultimate Challenge 1981

THE scene is the Park Hotel, Montrose, situated half-way
between Aberdeen and Arbroath on the red-stoned green-
tapestried landscape of Scotland's rich east coast.

A map of the Highlands is pinned on a wall, a desk is piled with
certificates and papers, and an unbureaucratic-looking lad sits
behind it, still in running strip. The spacious room is well supplied
with armchairs.

Eight miles west, a solitary figure is tramping along the soul/sole-
destroying road from Brechin. A passing milk lorry gives him a toot
and a wave, "The bloody steeple never seems to get nearer!" was no
original comment, though said with feeling as he later sprawled in
one of those armchairs, tea in hand, and lost in the vacuum feelings
of the end of a personal saga. The scene is the finishing point of the
annual Ultimate Challenge coast-to-coast marathon.

By lunchtime, downstairs is crowded too, with scantily-clad
youths downing welcome pints and scoffing huge platefuls from the
buffet, an odd sight as they are sitting next to tweedy-clad
committee ladies with their sherries and salads and sleek North Sea
Oil men.

About five parties have clocked in and, the initial shock of
finishing over, all want to talk at once as the memories of the last two
weeks rush back in trembling kaleidoscopic brilliance.

My quiet "dour-Scots" smile hid the fact that I found it rather
moving. Such uninhibited enjoyment in this dreich, grey world of
urban slavery is all too rare, quite apart from my being, in many
ways, responsible for the event.

I have enjoyed long tramps in the Highlands ever since I was old enough to pedal off into the wilds as a kid. For a dozen years we had done treks such as "The Road to the Isles" with Braehead School parties, long before the term "outdoor education" had been invented and the reality emasculated by bureaucracy.

People like John Hinde and Sandy Cousins had written about crossings and linkings of Munros, longitudinal and lateral. I had escaped my own bureaucratic pit to go off and traverse all the Munros in a single effort.

I had made a hottest-of-hot solo crossing in Jubilee Year, then repeated it one autumn with a friend, Ray Swinburn, who was to do the UC81 with a Fife friend called Ben-the-Burner (he worked in a crematorium). The solo crossing had taken in Munros galore; Ray's kept very much to valley rights-of-way, as it was the stalking season.

It was from these seeds that the idea of an "event" sprang. In many ways it is a "non event" because there is no set route, no competition and only the most basic of guideline rules. But it has encouraged people to dream dreams... and then put feet to them.

The summer hills are overcrowded, midge-infected and inevitably wet. By August, the walker is not welcomed. Easter is the lambing peak in these norther parts. May is usually a good month, clear of all these inconveniences and with B and B facilities and locals only too glad of some additional customers. Hence, the middle two weeks of May came to be the sacred dates for the Challenge. UC80 had not one wet day, UC81 rained only on the last afternoon—or at least that was how it went for Tony and I, (UC83 only had one dry day just to redress the balance as the next chapter tells.)

Scotland is pressurised continually by hamfisted southern bureaucracy (things like the artificial West Highland Way) so any scheme had to keep within hill traditions and methods. An "event" at all sounded anathema to many, but the experience has quietened most criticism.

Hoteliers, keepers, farmers, landowners, shopkeepers, in fact anyone met along the way, proved hospitable, helpful and kind. Anyone tackling an Ultimate Challenge is likely to be an experienced, friendly, tough type anyway.

The biggest single factor to be avoided was the danger of a lineal

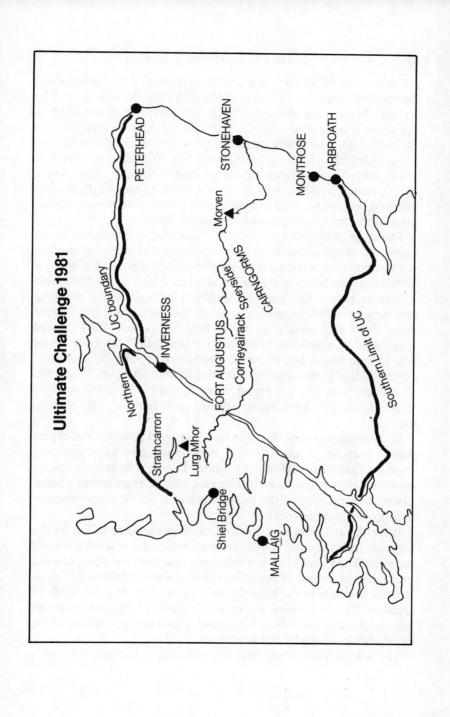

Ultimate Challenge 1981

PETERHEAD

STONEHAVEN

MONTROSE

ARBROATH

Morven

UC boundary

CAIRNGORMS

Corrieyairack speyside

INVERNESS

FORT AUGUSTUS

Northern

Strathcarron

Lurg Mhor

Southern Limit of UC

Shiel Bridge

MALLAIG

route developing which would lead to over use and all the polluting, destructive results we see on something like the Pennine Way. The intiative of planning had to be kept as well, so the start was given as the whole coastline between the head of Loch Carron and the head of Loch Ailort, to which was added Acharacle and Oban to give some alternatives for a more southerly line. The finish was the east coast, anywhere between Aberdeen and Arbroath, after which people simply reported in to Montrose. Nobody has yet declined to accept a certificate! And to help spread people even thinner on the ground the start is stretched over several days.

The style of crossing, its speed or lack of it, the numbers in the party, the route taken— all these are up to the participants. The word competitor is not used. Most of the starting points are popular West Highland hotels and they are often used for a touch of comfort overnight before the graft of backpacking and lonely camping commences—though some I could name managed a comfy roof every night and usually a midday hostelry as well. They walked roads though, a personal anethema, but that is their business. Those who take in twelve Munros or Corbetts qualify for a "High-Level" route. All this gives scope for returning again and again. You could do it every year and not repeat yourself, change from low to high-level efforts, go alone, camp entirely, not camp at all—and so on.

A tremendous esprit de corps has developed among Challengers partly because of the friendly, non-competitive spirit and the resulting socialising along the route. It seems everyone knows everyone after a few days. Trail news, gossip, romance blossoms. Locals become part of the game. Certain B and B places become unforgettable experiences.

It is still hard work and the first few days see some falling by the wayside, as bodies and spirits give way before the vast emptiness of the west. The Great Glen is a milestone and once the A9 is crossed only the most serious of accidents will stop anyone from crawling in. Routes are submitted beforehand and experts, like the staff of Outward Bound Lochiel, Roger Smith, Rennie McOwan or myself look at these to see they are sane and within the capabilities of the experience outlined by the applicants.

The wildness and toughness can still shatter though. It is not a

Tony at the Fords of Avon shelter on the 1981 Ultimate Challenge

game for the casual. A ceiling of 200 entries is set (human pollution is no prettier than any other) and this is just right. Tony and I only met other participants on three of our twelve days of walking and only Morven in Aberdeenshire of all our summits had people on it. That you can walk for days and see no-one else sometimes shocks the newcomer.

Geography (water especially) created a few bottlenecks at places like Fort Augustus or Dalwhinnie, Braemar or Glendoll, but this only briefly brings people together . . . for some memorable social meetings. A soft night in a hotel does not go amiss now and then. "Bath and bed" entries appear in many logbooks I'm sure—even if in one Braemar B and B the bath taps are chained and padlocked after 11 p.m.!

Planning is very much part of the game, but it is one aspect I miss in some ways as I know Scotland so well. By the time I've walked across I've already, in my mind's eye, worked out next year's route!

Tony and I started from Strathcarron Hotel in 1981 and for several days, wandered through the huge area of roadless, mountains eastwards. We walked for three days over five summits before we even saw another person or habitation. A traverse of all the Sgurr na Lapaich summits was curtailed because of a fierce wind (others had a thunderstorm) so we "bagged" An Socath only before dropping down to follow huge Loch Mullardoch to the dam. The locals call it "the Atlantic."

I had planned to leave food there, but as a B and B had opened in nearby Cozac Lodge we gladly used that. Bathed and clean, we sat to a scrumptious Danish cream tea, china all being delicate Copenhagen ware—a change from our tin dixis!

The next day produced a great cloud sea, but as we climbed on to the ridges of Affric for more Munros we had glorious sunshine above it. The sunshine won the next day for crossing the two ranges south and east to Fort Augustus (Loch Ness is a nuisance!) and rather than face miles of hot tarred road to Torgyle Bridge, we piled our ruckers into bivy bags and floated them ahead as we swam the great, black, peaty Moriston river. THAT went into trail gossip! The Military Road over the hill took us to Fort Augustus, named after Bloody Cumberland of '45 infamy.

With such fair weather we abandoned our tent for the Monadh Liath, but after reaching Corrieyairack Hill the clouds thickened and we descended to find a howff instead of a bivy among those now decimated Munros. At the Fort we had run into a Doncaster Wayfarers' quartet (four is the maximum group size) and other solitary parties.

At Laggan we found Ray and Ben, so they cancelled their Kingussie Youth Hostel night to join us at Milehouse hut and dinner at the Ossian Hotel, Kincraig, which some claim (and I won't dispute it) combines the best of food with the cheeriest service of any route across.

The next day we set off for a 27-mile day via the Lairig Ghru, Ben Macdhui and Loch Avon. After another hill-gathering circuit, we followed the Avon River down to where it suddenly bends north then worked through to Cock Bridge and Corgarff Castle. Luxury all the way now . . . from the friendly Cock Bridge Hotel on Donside we traversed Morven, our thirteenth summit, to Dinnet on Deeside to stay at the Glenlewis Hotel.

Linking Dee and North Esk are two of the historic Mounth passes, the Fungle and the Firmounth, both ending at Tarfside. We took the latter, because it was new to us and a great route and secondly, because it led to the Parsonage the only accommodation available in North Glen Esk.

Gladys Guthrie at the Parsonage is perhaps the event's fairy godmother for she (and her family) give the warm welcome and splendid food so dear to weary hikers. Tents on the lawn and three sittings for meals are taken in her stride. Many routes are "bent" to take in the Parsonage.

A tent and supplies waited for Tony and I, as we planned to keep to the hills and fields all the way to Stonehaven with one night out en route. We had walked the long tarred, hard miles out from the Angus glens before.

We groped through cloud over to near Bridge of Dye, but it cleared for the unforgettable Tippermuir hills beyond, only to rain hard once we reached the sprawling forest. Miles of its Turkish bath atmosphere had us ready to camp. Alas, tent up, we crawled in to find we had pitched on top of a swarming ants' nest—not the first time I've done that but, hopefully the last.

We scoffed the tea that had been brewing while we pitched, struck camp, donned our rain gear again and went on—and on and on—till at 10 p.m. we came down out of clawing clouds to the subdued lights of Stonehaven and the sea: Ultimate Challenge 81 was over. The next day I spent at Montrose. It was marvellously cheerful and rewarding, meeting old friends and making new ones. Second only to the excited tales of UC81 were the extravagant dreams for UC82.

The Ultimate Challenge continues, year by year, to provide great enjoyment—whatever the weather. The average age of participants is 43 and every year has seen several septuagenarians complete the trek. It is quite a committment of holiday time so those doing it are out to enjoy life. It is also a genuine financial injection to the local economy—something, pubs apart, to which the weekender seldom contributes. As one keeper told me "When the cuckoos come I know the Challengers won't be far behind". Anyone interested in the Ultimate Challenge can obtain information (large SAE please) from UC Organiser, 16 Glenbo Drive, Denny, Stirlingshire.

13. Ardnamurchan to Buchan Ness

A Cornish friend was most put out to discover that Ardnamurchan Point was thirty miles west of Land's End, the last rocky flourish of mainland Britain with only a symphony of islands beyond. It is a natural starting point for a walk across Scotland and what could be more natural than to finish at Buchan Ness, Scotland's most easterly point?

But what a dreich, dank spring to choose for my journey. Any walk across a country gives a cross-section view and it would be a good thing (especially in an election year) if all prospective MPs were required to walk the width of the land on foot before opening their mouths. Nothing shows the state of a country so clearly. The farmer lambing in the rain certainly has views to express.

Ardnamurchan to Buchan Ness is very much a rural walk. Ellon was the biggest place I met on the way across. Probably the deepest impression is of friendly people, suffering livestock, and the continuous discourtesy of the weather. Not for nothing was the tune running in my head day after day called "Land of the Mountain and the Flood." Scott knew Scotland. He also sailed on coasts to visit lighthouses, a tenuous link with this stravaig, for both start and finish were marked by the friendly presence of lights. There are few ugly lighthouses.

Ardnamurchan's I first saw in a gale, fighting round it in the dark, while a hundred feet aloft being seasick over the sails we were stowing. It was nice to take most of a day by the local bus from the Corran Ferry to Kilchoan and then stroll on with the first cuckoos flitting about (with voices yet unpolished) to reach the golden western extremity. In the walled garden primroses spread in clumps large as eiderdowns. Offshore the eider ducks called "Oh! Oh!" like disapproving grandmothers. Eigg and Rhum were lithoed on the horizon. Here, indeed, one could know in the words of Shelley, "The pleasure of believing all we see is boundless." That night I slept out under the stars and watched them wheel through the frosty hours. They were the last stars of the walk.

Ardnamurchan has changed over the years. Every house now seems to have been rebuilt, even remote crofts in remote bays. One of the bays meant a hard new track over an old pony path and later on the muddiness of a forestry road indicated different use. There were improvements all right. The first shepherd I met moaned about the lack of rain. The ground was hard and the burns down to trickles—while the rest of the land had had the wettest April since records began. It was a day of blues and greens, the sky and fields coloured as sharply as footballers' strips.

The hotel in Acharacle had left out breakfast so I could be off at an unearthly hour. There was food enough for ten! The helpfulness and quality of hotels and bed and breakfast places was another memory of the trip. This is not just a case of economics demanding competitive service. It is part of a good tradition. Only two weeks earlier, in Somerset, I had been turned away, late at night because I was alone and they "only had double rooms."

I had set off early as I planned to traverse Ben Resipol and spend a night in a remote bothy. The old path along Loch Shiel has been largely destroyed by new afforestation. A promised replacement is waited with some cynicism. I eventually scrambled up a deep gorge on the west side of the hill to reach a high loch where we had some tea and left the rucksack, then went up to the top of the hill. It is one of the best viewpoints in Scotland with an incomparable mixture of rugged land and smooth seas and sky. A high level traverse took us over and down by the holes and filleted stratas above Strontian. Lead from the mines here tipped the bullets fired at Waterloo and now the big diggers are in, preparing sites, and roads and water supplies for the opening of the works once more.

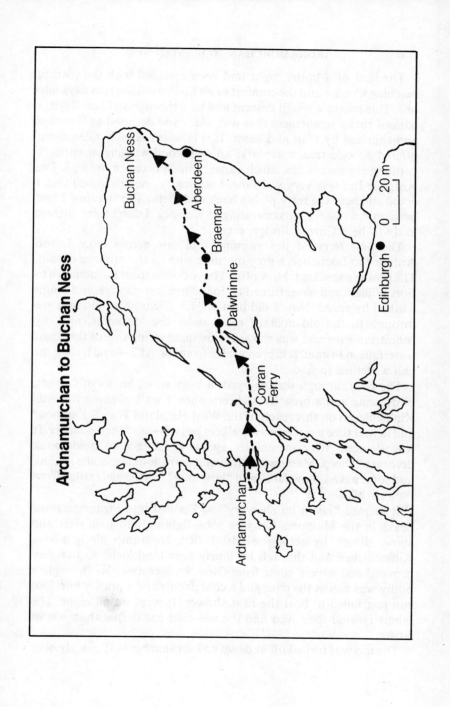

Ardnamurchan to Buchan Ness

Buchan Ness

Aberdeen

Braemar

Dalwhinnie

Corran
Ferry

Ardnamurchan

Edinburgh

0   20 m

The idea of a bothy night had been replaced with the plan of reaching Corran and the comfort of an hotel: running two days into one. This meant a rough descent and hike through to Glen Gour, a pass of rocky remoteness that was silent and deserted as if cursed and shunned by man and beast. It was weird. Slowly Glen Gour offered an odd tree, a skylark, an owl wood-winding, a curlew's curdling cry and lambs which came running between my legs. The Ardgour Inn was very welcome. I was early enough in bed that I could still hear the ferry plying back and forth. The last time I had been on the vessel it was operating at Kessock. I don't think there is likely to be a Corran Bridge, ever.

The first ferry of the morning took me across from Island Ardgour to Lochaber, a grey morning with all the promise of rain. The promise was kept. How often I have driven from Ballachulish to Fort William and never turned off to Inchree, car-captive, and brain-washed by speed. Now I did turn off, for Glenrigh would take me through to the old military road under the Mamores, and my pedestrian slowness was rewarded by discovering one of the finest waterfalls in Britain. It is even visible from the A82—and it took me half a lifetime to find.

The pass through was enjoyed: a back wind, banks of flowers, birds' song and a brew by a cheery burn. I walked along towards Kinlochleven on this reach of the West Highland Way for an hour and in that time a dozen way-walkers passed—and then no more. It was Pennine Way mentalities again: a rat-race of guide-book decorated sheep. Many were lame and sorry-looking, some ill-clad, and some asked "how far?" and "how long?" as the hail rattled from the raw hills.

It seemed "just a bit showery" so I pulled up to traverse some peaks in the Mamores but was soon fighting into hail, sleet and snow, driven by strong winds. I fled, to tramp along above Kinlochleven and through by lonely loon-loud lochs to the grey drovers' and reivers' route from Glen Nevis eastwards. The night's bothy was across the river and a cold paddle and a prickly barefoot run just failed to beat the next shower. It went on all night. The lambs bleated their woe and the wet-cold cut deeper than winter frosts.

The tap was turned off at dawn so I scrammbled off quickly over the Penny Pass as it is called (pennies are left by the cairns on top) to the Lairig Leacach, another old route down which cattle from Skye and the West came tramping to the far markets of Crieff, Falkirk and even Smithsfield. We made tea in the hut there and watched the scudding clouds. The big hills of "This Yin" and "That Yin" were swopped for the rocky bumps of Cruach and Sgurr Innse and then we wended down Coire Lair. A sad number of dead lambs littered the valley.

When we cut over the shoulder of hill to come down to Loch Treig we became aware of a buzzing sound and this turned out to be the Scottish Six-Day Trials: bikes were coming up to Fersit and up the hillside beyond to do tests in a rocky gorge before going on to Loch Ossian. There were hundreds of cars in attendance.

I woke to a woodpecker at work just outside and the cuckoos were working their early shift. My walk to Ossian soon ran into the muddy furrows left by all the bikes so walking was without rhythm and vile. Blackcock were about, burbling at their *lek*, and roe deer had left their tracks on top of the grid pattern of the hundred tyres. By barking back at one roe deer I lured him over the skyline but one look was enough and he was off like the wind. What a deadly predator man must be that all wild things flee at the sight of him!

The path was unpleasant enough that I changed my route and cut down to cross Strath Ossian to follow up a burn into the hills beyond: a fine sweeping array running East-West yet oddly without a collective name. My traverse of Beinn Eibheinn, Aonach Beag, Geal Charn, and Carn Dearg was the biggest hill day I was to have but by leaving my pack at the cols between the end ones the foot-poundage was reduced a bit. On a big walk you fight every ounce of the way.

I thought I might have had trouble crossing a river beyond but it proved easy enough and by the River Pattack I passed a comfortable night in a bothy in a small wood. There was not a breath of wind and the fire was soon blazing without the usual kippering smoke. Boots and stockings soon dried off for the tops had been cloudy and wet. Northern rims still leaned out in fierce cornices.

In the small wood I counted 17 dead hinds and all through the walk the death-toll had been far higher than usual. Disease as well as starvation seems to have been at work. Not enough deer are being culled and when they are not shot, they starve—an aspect the sentimental tend to forget.

I reached the A9 (always a great landmark on a coast-to-coast hike) by the Fara, a cairn-topped sprawl of hill above Loch Ericht and Dalwhinnie which few walkers go up as it is not over the magic Munro altitude of 3,000 ft. It is a grand viewpoint—normally—I had a bank of cloud and hurried off down through the Dirc Mhor, a strange cut of a pass with cliff walls and tumbling screes and no burn. The burn came out at the foot, in full flow, and wended off to meet the Wade Road at Dalwhinnie. It made a pleasant brew-spot before returning to the hurly-burly of traffic.

We set off east the next morning in a cold, wet wind to tramp through to the Gaick Pass, one of the great old North-South routes from long before tarred roads and even pre-General Wade. From the Corran Ferry to Dalwhinnie I had not walked along tarred roads and from the A9 it took several days to break through to Braemar and tarred roads again. This wilderness quality is what makes Scotland so different, and attractive, to walkers accustomed to the more crowded hills of Snowdonia or Lakeland.

A few miles on I suddenly leapt into the air and off the path—an adder lay on it in a watery patch of sunlight. It was sluggish and probably regretted coming out of hibernation. I left the sandpiper-ringing river to pull up to the pass through to Glen Feshie.

I had intended a high crossing of the Cairngorms to Cock Bridge but it was snowing hard the next morning and I had to take the 25 miles of low-level walking to Braemar instead. The bridge from the Tilt path had been washed away years ago and there were others shown which do not exist: black marks for the OS in these conditions—when it can become a matter of life and death. I met a walker later on who had fallen in—as he put it, "ass over tilt"—and been swept away. The Linn o' Dee was churning like a mill with a whisky-tinted power of water going through. I walked down to Mar Lodge hoping for some tea.

There, however, all had changed. There was nothing for the public. Even the popular campsite by the Lui had been ploughed up and planted. House after house was boarded up and empty, falling into decay. Braemar has no campsite (it now has) and minimal room

Ardnamurchan, furthest-west corner of Mainland Britain, and often the start of a coast-to-coast trek across to Buchan Ness, near Peterburgh

to expand, a feudal set-up which has little part of the late twentieth century, yet has strangled the village for decades. I headed for the youth hostels: hot showers made a change from cold paddles. When I phoned Kinloss for a forecast for the Eastern Cairngorms they asked if I had been in the hills that day and when I said yes, they gave the reply "Well, what you had today, you'll probably get again tomorrow."

By the time the snow started I was half a day through the hills. I wandered along by Braemar Castle and the beautiful old military bridge at Invercauld and then followed tracks up to Culardoch. The deer were all down at forest level but I was obviously gaining eastwards as hares were dashing about all day long. They were still changing back to summer colours. By Loch Builg the snow began and came down in gigantic dollops.

In minutes the landscape was changing from greys and browns to uniform white. We paddled rivers down to the gorge of the River Avon but instead of following it north we turned sharp right, east, along what may have been its original line. A trickle was the infant Don. We followed it several miles out to Cock Bridge and the Allergue Arms.

My bedroom window looked across to Corgarff Castle; a grey tower set against greyer skies. It had been used by Montrose, was an arsenal during the '45, and a garrison was maintained there till well into the 1800s. My day's walk down Donside took me from Corgarff Castle to Kildrummy Castle but I remember little about it as it rained most of the way. I had to force myself to stop past Strathdon, with its graceful old Pollullie Bridge, and make some tea.

I spent the night at Malt Croft Farm at Milltown of Kildrummy and arrived in time to join the men at supper: a mouth-watering fish soup, thick as porridge, and braised liver and onions. We sat before a peat fire and watched endless replays of Aberdeen's victory over Real Madrid.

At Bridge of Alford I deserted the Don to strike across to Keig and the first shop I had found open on the walk. After greedy indulgence I wandered up towards Bennachie and lunched under big beeches at a den called My Lord's Throat. A gap under the Mither Tap really felt like the end to the hill country but before reaching

Inverurie I was ambushed by three thunderstorms. On each occasion I found shelter so kept dry. It was like watching a battle on TV rather than facing real bullets.

The Banks of Ury Hotel apologised that they only did bedroom Continental-style breakfasts but this was useful. I made my tea and slipped off at six o'clock. My map had the east coast on it. The sky was blue.

The early start meant I reached Pitmedden at opening time for the NTS gardens, 9.30 a.m. Their formal seventeenth-century lay-out rather lacked colour in May but the fountain allowed me to fill my dixi and have a brew in the picnic corner with an admiring audience of Jacob's sheep. I then tramped into Ellon and on to meet the coast at Cruden Bay. When I dodged into the Inn there to avoid a thunder shower I found a friend at the bar and as he lived across the road this gave an enjoyable end to the crossing. While he and some other friends went off climbing I wandered along the cliffs to Buchan Ness. There are some good features like the Bullers of Buchan where a huge hole leads out to the sea by a tunnel, or Slains Castle, the inspiration for Count Dracula's Castle.

It had been a rough crossing but the toughness itself is rewarding. You still get out of life what you put into it. The other, sadder refrain, was on the devastation of life, both wild and tame, due to the long, cold, wet spring. Life, being such a tennous thing, is to be lived richly. A Scottish "walk about" yields coin of gold.

*That furthest-west to furthest-east crossing was my
UC83 trip, the only one I have done alone, but unless I
actually mentioned it, there is nothing to indicate it was
part of an event—which is how we want it. For fun
participants can send in accounts of their wanderings
and* The Great Outdoors *magazine (which with* Ultimate
Equipment *actually sponsors the event) prints the best
High Level and best Low Level story in the November
issue, which also gives the first details of the following
year's event.*

*The next two articles are also about crossings, very
different in their demands and in character, but I hope
showing the same enjoyment. The hills are so good to us
in that we can all, irrespective of age, sex, fragility or
anything else, be enriched from our wanderings into the
wilds. Not many pleasures are so wholly good.*

14. Across Sutherland and Caithness

JUNE 22: **North of Suilven**

Yesterday the radio moaned about Britain's wettest solstice in a
quarter of a century but there was no rain in Sutherland. It had
been a rather frantic day: climbing Ben Hope early (before the gale)
and laying food caches as we zig-zagged up and down endless single
track roads (with or without passing places) before finally ending at
Inverkirkaig for a sociable night with Stan Bradshaw.

Stan and I had last been together climbing Toubkal, at 4167
metres the highest peak in North Africa. Here it was Suilven filled
our talk and caught our eyes as we leant on the wind for a pre-
nightcap dander out to the point looking over the Minch to the
Hebrides. Summer pipers (nothing "common" about these herlads
of the spring) flitted about and buzzed the dog who was much more
interested in rabbits than baby birds.

The gale was still galloping over the bony wilderness today and I
rather trembled to be setting off to walk across the "wildest and
best" of Scotland. Most big winds end in big wettings. Beyond
Suilven is a country of perpetual savageness—without any weather
tantrums added.

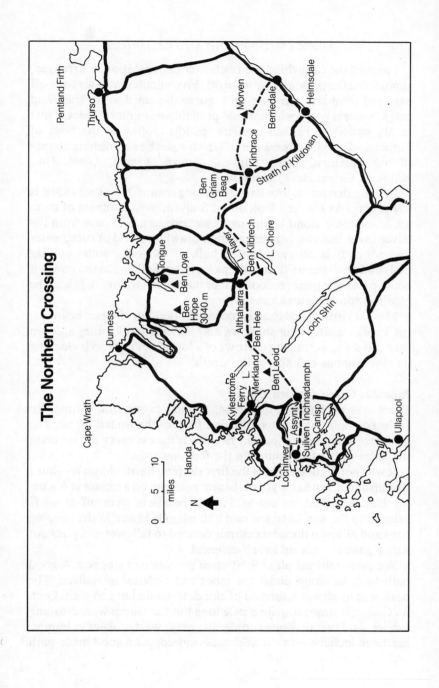

The Northern Crossing

I parked the car behind the Lochinver police station as arranged, shouldered the pack and we were off. Five minutes later we were off map-red road and wending up a gorge, hemmed in by trees and crags, a secret wood which would probably be our last. Trees, if met at all, would be ranked conifers, puddle-footing in the bogs of Sutherland and Caithness out of which rose the astonishing shapes of our northern peaks: Suilven, Canisp, Assynt, Leoid, Hee, Klibreck, Griam Beag, Morven.

Linking that lot on foot has been a long dream. Now (in 1985) it is happening. As I write I look out at Suilven, most stunning of them all. It suddenly stood before us as we topped a wee pass from the River Inver into this bigger, rougher, brawling world of rock, water and wind. It is an exaggerated hulk of hill—like some bulging bodybuilder—but its flexed biceps leave no doubt as to the punch it could pack. We prefer to look rather than touch today. A gale in the glen will mean a hurricane up there.

My last visit outside found golden light flooding the glen below us, the knolls casting long shadows and the sun spotlighting a dozen deer splashing across the narrows of a lochan. A cuckoo is clocking its monotonous call across the strath.

June 23: Green Garden Country

There was no harm in dreaming, as long as we won through to Inchnadamph today where the first food cache waited for us. The hardness of a planned journey like this is the necessity for covering the miles rather than climbing the feet upwards.

It was not a good night—the first sleeping hard seldom is—but I was up and down like a yo-yo: Storm pounced on a mouse at 4 a.m., my bladder called me out at 5 a.m., the alarm went off at six (I listened to the wind and the rain and snuggled back in the sleeping bag) and at seven the water carrier decided to fall over and pour out half a gallon. I got up in self-defence!

We eventually set off at 9.30 when the rain had stopped. A good path took us along under the moorland pedestal of Suilven. The peak was hidden in a turmoil of cloud. It would have to wait. Loch na Gainimh was not quite a mile long but the waves were crashing ashore and white horses rode its grey waste. Rocky bumps, scattered lochans—this is wilderness indeed, yet a good made-path allowed us to tramp east at a great rate. A narrow gut of gorge ("The Dark Glen") led through to Lochan Fada ("The Fair Loch") and from half way along it we began to contour upwards steadily to gain the lower levels of Canisp which we had felt rather than seen. A waterfall spilling over a crag above a wind-free hollow called for an early lunch brew.

As soon as we crept up to the lip of the fall we entered a new, wide-horizoned world. Storm was led off by a grouse doing a broken wing act, several deer tiptoed across the skyline and a fleeting shadow suddenly resolved into a swooping golden eagle—just 100 yards away. When I turned to follow its flight I saw Suilven was jagging out from the clouds. Cameras, quick!

The rucksack was left and we sped up, pushed by the wind, to try Canisp. The final cone never did clear but Suilven was there, grey on greys, shot silver now and then by touches of sun. We were quite sorry to swing round and down the quartz miles to the River Lonan that drains down to Inchnadamph and Loch Assynt.

Just two days ago I'd left a food dump by the Allt nan Uamh near the Fish Hatchery and while still half-a-mile off I could hear a strident bell ringing from the hatchery. It went on and on: an alarm of some kind shrilling to a Sabbath-silent world. I cursed it for all the nearby wind-free camping places were within sound. It could go on all night! So I had to go upstream and camp in the tight valley—a bit of a wind tunnel.

Tins galore and fresh vegetables ensured a good meal. Later we wandered up to see the resurgence of the river. The natural line is suddenly dry; all the water pours out of the side wall of the glen. It is weird, but the whole area is riddled with burns which vanish and appear in peculiar fashion. The 1:50,000 map only hints at some. It is the best of Scotland for the modern caveman. The evening cheered up for the sun went down over Canisp, shining in the tent door and countering the chill wind off the big Assynt hills of tomorrow. When I wrote the first paragraph this morning it was in a spirit of gloom. Now I feel much better. The first empty quarter has been passed, even a hill climbed—and the sun shines for the last drink of the night.

June 24: The Ascent to Assynt

Today in many ways was the crux of the crossing (to borrow a climbing term) and having it now behind is both a relief to the soul and a glad resting of the soles. Ben More Assynt, 998 metres, is the highest summit of the crossing and the descent off it led, not to the security of a road but into one of the bleakest of wastelands imaginable. The tent stands 1,000 feet up on a green shelf of grass by a burn. Its waters actually flow to the East coast yet we are closer to the western sea here than we were two nights ago under Suilven, for two big fiords, bridged spectacularly now at Kylesku, cut deep into the grey hills: Loch Glencoul and Loch Glendhu. Everything drains into them, except for this vast hollow, fifteen miles round which drains south to Glen Cassley and eventually into the Kyle of Sutherland.

I am particularly glad to be over the main drain for a dozen years ago I came off Ben More Assynt in a monsoon deluge that had the rivers rising into dramatic spate. I had to strip and ford the Cassley waist deep—half an hour later it would have been impassable. At one stage I thought that desperate day was going to be repeated.

The brilliance of sun, and no wind, woke me at 5 but I snoozed till 6 and set off at 7. What a difference that last hour would have made. Early hours should always be grabbed if not for necessity, then for the "fierce joy of living," and the balm of coolness and an earlier arrival. It is early in the day that we see most wildlife.

The first hour in the sun was a sweat-bath across heather moors pockmarked with sink-hole craters. I changed into shorts while Storm investigated a badger set but we eventually hit the river we wanted. It was a good sized burn really but all at once it swung up against a crag and vanished gurgling into the ground. Perhaps it is the one which pops out two miles away to pass last night's campsite?

We had a brew at the rucker and in just the twenty minutes of relaxing the sky changed from ninety per cent blue to one hundred per cent cloudy while a wall of wet was advancing up Loch Assynt. "Too bright too soon will rain by noon." The rain came as a saturating smir, still without wind, so I just draped my waterproof over my pack. We wended up to the Bealach Breabag, under Conival, one of the finest passes in Scotland, both as a through-route and for its structure and scenery. For its flowers too: cornel, thrift, mantles, globeflower, roseroot, starry saxifrage, violets, thyme, even daisies and dandelions were about our feet as we edged under cliffs for the mossy gap and the red screes beyond.

The SE Ridge of Conival sweeps up in craggy steps but I wanted something new so carried on round into Garbh Choire *the rough corrie*. A name like that usually means it and here the headwall is a shambles of scree while the scoured bottom just fails to have a glacier-scooped lochan. We sheltered under a boulder for lunch, then zig-zagged up steep grass east of the screes to gain the lofty ridge connecting Conival and its biggar brother Ben More of Assynt. These were visited in turn. I seemed to float over the mist-slippery quartz without the drag of the rucksack. Storm exploded a grenade of ptarmigan chicks.

We baled off down the other side of the linking ridge and, coming out of the mist, set one lot of deer after another high-stepping along the slopes. It was three miles down to the river but another was added because of the constant bog and water deviations. There was a ration of ups in the downhill too. A sair pech, and a slaistery pech.

The centre of that vast hollow is covered by two lochs: Gorm Loch Mor and Fionn Loch Mor. They were neither *gorm* nor *fionn*, just *liath*, and connected by a river a third of a mile long which might or might not be fordable but almost at once I found a spot where it was possible to boulder-hop across. That deserved tea as a relief: sweet, milky Earl Grey. All the rimming hills were covered in cloud and the drizzle had saturated the grass. We began the long haul up the Fionn Allt towards our escape pass of the morrow and found our secret sward a mile up.

June 25: By Beinn Leoid and Ben Hee

A mix of soft moss and grey stone led us up to *Beinn Leoid*. Inside the wall round the trig point was a flourish of delicate wood sorrel. Outside were whole mats and rugs of thrift, including one white one. As we charged down out of the mist we set some deer scampering. All day, every day, there are deer, too many to record. We had tea by Loch Dubh after the path contoured down off the pass. Leoid refused to clear. It still would not clear as we traversed along to

break over a ridge to pick up a stalkers' path down to the deep gash
of the next motorable glen.

The houses of Kinloch stood solitary with Loch More and Arkle
beyond. The tiny, single-tracked A838, seemed an apology for
mechanical intrusion. What a fastness this area must have been in
the bad old days, though perhaps then there would be houses and
shielings where I walked in a deserted wilderness.

A string through Storm's collar and we ambled up the road to
Loch Merkland. We have now walked right across and off Sheet 15.
Sheet 16 we unearthed from roadside boulders. Mice had been at the
cache in just the few days it had been there and a carton of juice was
no more. It was too early to camp (2 pm) so I ate a tin of raspberries,
a tin of custard and some other weighty goodies before shouldering
a heavy pack again. After a total of 1½ miles of road I swung off up
an estate track through the Bealach nam Meirleach *The Robbers
Pass* and then round the skirts of Ben Hee to camp at a loch below its
NE cliffs. A peat bank acted as a wind break for the loch was lively.
Ben Hee is a huge pile of bulging tops. If the weather allows we can
sclim it the morn's morn.

The wind dropped after supper and now I write with an anti-
midge coil on "just in case." Earlier the air sizzled with flights of
insects. midge-sized, but harmless. Maybe they were male midges—
only the female bites! A fish plops in the loch occasionally and the
water is edged with spearwort in flower. The view is out to Klibreck
and the Griams—three days of walking to the next horizon. Grey
and raw as November, the rain only persists now when we are snug
in bed. Today really has given a surge eastwards, the jumble of
peaks is behind, the more spacious landscape ahead.

Apart from road traffic on that 1½ miles I have not seen anyone
since Lochinver. You could not walk four days alone in many
countries. This loch is Loch Coire na Saidhe Duibhe—*the loch of
the corrie of the black hay.* Maybe it should be *saidh*, meaning *bitch*
or the *prow* of a ship.

June 26: Ben Hee and Ben Klibreck
A northern farmer was once asked what the climate was like up
there. The reply was a shake of the head. "I don't know much about
climate now but it's certain we get plenty of weather." Today gave a

Storm, the Munro-bagger, on the trig-point of Ben Hope in Sutherland

pretty good example of weather. I doubt if it stayed the same for more than an hour or two at a time.

It began sunny and bright so after half a breakfast and the first midge bite we romped off, unladen, for Ben Hee. A path led from the loch's outflow up to a bold buttress but we cut up its flank under a line of cliffs to have a look at the climbing potential. Ben Hee has twin summits and the lower had to be traversed to reach the higher. The cloud rolled in as we rounded the impressive ridge to the top. It seemed to be a personal spite for I had hardly finished the second half breakfast when it cleared again. It was steam-drying rather than turning wet however and Klibreck churned out cloud like a volcano. A four-mile path along the flank of the ridge, Druim nam Bad, led to the wee road from Altnaharra to Ben Hope. "Bad" was probably an apt word. The symbol for bog was spread over fifteen grid squares! It was grilling-hot but windless and grey.

Ben Hope and Ben Loyal had come into view yesterday afternoon. First one, then the other dominated the view today as we gained miles eastwards. Klibreck is a huge sprawl with a certain brutal symmetry. The four miles of road saw it clearing at last to fill the view ahead.

I sat on a knoll outside Altnaharra to sort out a parcel and prepare a packet for home with finished film, maps, etc. With two days' food on board I had a hefty rucksack. I phoned home, posted things, and actually spoke to a lad with his dog. He said, "Aye, how goes it?" and I said, "Aye, warm." It was verra hot and we crossed the moors towards the wall of Klibreck in a lather of sweat. Sixty or more deer were traversing high on the hill.

Originally we had planned to stay overnight at Altnaharra. As the only "place" of the journey it even had the temptation of a hotel but it was too early in the afternoon so we wended on. When I found we were on the lower slopes of Klibreck, well, we climbed it. Because it was there, between us and the east coast, a menace of a Munro, a black cloud-gatherer that might be foul on the morrow. Tell it not in Gath but we had the summit clear. Just. It clouded over five minutes after we had left the top.

I was determinned to have a midge-free camp so high on Klibreck seemed a safe place. On the last zig (or zag) of path there was a fortuitous gush of water so I filled my carrier. This yellow object was useful for locating my belongings in the mist, for it was one and a half miles from the top. A wee bump remained before we dropped to the col before The Whip, the last bump of the Klibreck collection. The tent was just up in time. A shower came scudding over from Ben Armine. It soon passed, then the wind changed to blow in the tent door. You can't win!

We are pitched high above Loch Naver and beyond the moors behind it rises the carbuncle mass of Ben Loyal: a view of sweeping grandeur. If every joint aches it is worth it. Obadiah talked about a "nest among the stars". This is mine.

June 27: Step We Wetly On We Go

I was ready for off at 7.30 when the heavens opened. "Soon go off," I told the dog and we "cooried doon" a while. It did not go off for over two hours by which time I felt very cold. I heated a can of soup and then took down the tent. We groped our way through tearing cloud down hillsides which were exploding rivers out of springs and pools. The option of staying put was not practicable as I was low in Gaz.

We came below cloud level and across Loch Choire could see all the burns were white-foaming torrents. This at once revised my plans for no river-crossing would be safe for many hours. Loch Choire exits as the River Mallart and I'd planned to go down its left bank on a path and ford it where it turned north to Loch Naver. We would then head east outside plantations to the succession of lochs beyond which lay my cache under Ben Griam Mor. As fording was out of the question I just hoped a bridge shown would let us on to the right bank.

Our feet were saturated by the time we reached the valley. For most of the day the rain was a dreary dribble—enough to keep waterproofs on and so swelter along. It had been fun in the deluge on high but squelshing miles of spongy bog were simply tedious and exhausting. A mere stream flowing in before the forest forced us to back-track quarter of a mile before we could leap across. We had a coffee to cheer us up and spiced Moroccan sardines were warming. Saturated ploughed land was as near as I could describe the next mile. It took nearly an hour. Beyond that the same again should have led to a track but on topping a rise it was to see it all under trees.

Rude things were said about the Forestry Commission and the Ordnance omission.

The only interesting moment was when a strange deer trotted past us. It never saw us and went by in graceful bounds. It was neither red deer nor roe. I hope it originated in the tundra rather than arid regions. Maybe it had webbed feet.

We sloshed up drains and over the corrugations and were relieved to see the track still existed. A mile on there was a deer fence across the path. No stile. Storm found it an awkward climb. Two miles on and with a car seen on the B871 ahead, I had a look at the map and, horrors, found my compass had gone. We left the rucker and walked back to the deer fence without finding it. An hour later I was back at the rucksack feeling pretty dank in spirit. No compass could mean no Morven, the Caithness flourish to end the Sutherland days. I felt tired and bad tempered. We cringed in the lee of a bridge and drank tea till the stove ran out of fuel. Four or five miles of road walking at that stage was cruel. It was like the opening sentence of John Buchan's first novel: "Before me stretched a black heath over which the mist blew in gusts, and through whose midst the road crept like an adder."

The weather at last hung itself out to dry. Ben Griam Mor cleared and our food and fuel lay by the roadside below it. Away beyond rose a fang in the grey—Morven the mighty.

A biscuit tin of perishables and a carrier bag of tinned food had been hidden in roadside rubble (Altnaharra's had been in a nettle patch!) and just two hundred yards away was some close-cropped heather on an alluvial bank: the perfect site. A safe, dry pitch in that world of wet and wilderness was enough to revive the spirits.

The view back over loch after loch to the black cloud-draped Klibreck group was like something from the Arctic. The weather felt that way too: a cold drizzle and a chill wind. The sleeping bag was relished. Supper in bed. You don't have that sort of service in a hotel. Today we walked off Sheet 16. Sheet 17, from the cache, is the last. The evening went in studying it. Just how would we tackle Morven without a compass? Tomorrow will tell.

This is proving as tough a crossing as I expected. It surprises people when I tell them this sort of thing is much harder than trekking in Atlas or Andes or Himalayas. It is as rewarding for that very reason and when conditions deign to smile, when feet are dry and belly full, why, it is the best there is.

28 June: Morven Ahoy!

"Slow and easy goes far in a day," Moleskin Joe says in "Children of the Dead End" and I applied this quite consciously today. It works! Mind you the weather helped: the first reasonable day we had had. It was a delight to dry everything before setting off. A gentle mile saw us up to a wide col under Ben Griam Mor and away over a roll of hills a real peak jabbed into the sky. It could only be Morven but it looked so far away—fourteen miles as the fly crows. Would we ever climb it?

The Eileag Burn had grassy verges in a sea of brown bog, the natural, easy route to follow despite the books always saying we must never follow streams. The only *never* as far as I'm concerned is "Never have rules." (The hills always find a way round any rule). "Experience is the sum of near misses" as the French say.

Where the burn became broad and deep before golden-edged Loch Arichline Storm had an escapade. A duck went scooting off along the water followed by eight or so young ones. The dog thought this most interesting and scampered along the bank watching the birds rather than where he was going. There was a bite out of the bank and Storm, in best Disney style, shot off the edge. He came up spluttering and indignant.

There was still enough water running off the hills to follow down and cross a high pedestrian suspension bridge outside Kinbrace. Between it and the road I managed to go over the top of both boots. Storm's turn to laugh. The cache nearby was rather a big one but we left a biscuit tin of goodies by the road (in a passing place) in hope that someone will find it. As we were about to tuck in to lunch a figure wended off the moor. He turned out to be a Halifax lad, the first person I actually chatted to properly since the Bradshaws at the start.

There was only the one range of hills between us and the sea but their initial tops held a weird splattering of a hundred lochans. We made a gentle route up to skirt them all and when Morven suddenly appeared again it was near and big: a great matronly boob shape (the Pap of Glencoe is nubile in comparison) which dominated everything around. We could see back as far as Klibreck and Loyal and here and there sweeps of rain hazed the clarity of a day of towering cumulus and a ration of blue.

At one stage I turned a step into a frantic leap (quite an effort with a hefty pack), otherwise I would have stood on an adder. All across I've been a bit worried about them for Storm's sake. He spends most of his time rushing along with nose to ground and could so easily run into one. It was a testimony to a better day that this handsome sluggard was out. He made no threat and when I waved and stamped he simply tried to curl up into a bowline. Nobody has been able to explain why some areas have adders and others don't. There is no obvious common denominator for their presence.

At the end of the great upland morass a green burn channel gave a camp site. It neatly frames Morven behind a couple of barren swellings in the ridge. We are as close as that, and the tent is pitched a couple of hundred yards into Caithness. Two deer came up the burn and were greatly puzzled by the tent.

29 June: Morven the Mighty

Morven the Magnificent. Those sound like titles to some awful Hollywood movie. The peak, however, deserves the titles: it is an extraordinary place.

Two or three miles of skirting along the intermediary bumps brought us to the col below the peak. I had some coffee and tried not to look at the peak but Morven stayed fiercely steep. It was a conical pile of conglomerate sandstone and this gave a shock to the acid sterility of the normal vegetation. Cloudberry, alpine ladies mantle, blaeberry, azalea, fir club moss, St John's wort, even rowans were growing on a feet-deep pile of moss and heather.

Few summits make one feel so airborne, or spread the world so like a map below. I could even see Dunnet Head and Orkney but, better yet, west, beyond Klibreck and Hee, beyond Assynt, there were the paps of Suilven. "My beginning was in my end," to misquote.

It was piercing cold with sweeping showers veiling half a dozen areas at once. We left when I could no longer stand the chill. Deer tracks skirted the huge cone of hill and then a peat-held stream took us to an estate road at a place called Wag. It ran down the Langwell Valley in easy fashion.

The sky grew black and I turned off up a stream just in time to raise the tent before the rain exploded on us. It gave a burst at full blast for half an hour and saw the day away in dreich rawness. Scaraben is my view through the rain and for once we lie on ordinary grass. A wren reels outside the tent—such quantity of sound from so small a mite.

30 June: Berriedale the Bountiful

Today was a brief coda, filling the walk across Northern Scotland into a full, very satisfying, symphony. The third sheet of map has new been crossed. There was no hurry to rise after a night of wet and cold but at seven the sun shone hotly into our bellyfold of hills. The wren still sang. The burn was high and inky dark.

The Langwell Valley grew richer with every step, the banks with old alders and the flanks bright with birch woods. I was wondering about the site of a ruined broch only to discover I was standing on top of it.

We crossed one of the many footbridges, with deer grazing on both banks, and crossed back at a simple but graceful 1866 cast iron bridge, which I hope will long be treated as the treasure it is.

The whole glen had been unusually tidy and, entering the real policies of the estate, it became apparent that a great deal of attention had been given to both landscape and buildings for a long time. It was particularly heartening to see a large area of newly planted oaks while the drive down to the A9 was a delight of many species—and many planted in the last forty years. The first thing I came on was a big walled garden and as it was all labelled, presumably open to the public. The door was not locked so I went in and wandered round while Storm sat by the rucksack. It was formally divided up by tall hedges but each section was different. There were even practical things like cabbages being grown! A new heath and alpine area was my favourite. A garden was a strange contrast after such barren days of walking.

I was just shouldering my pack when a couple appeared—and we greeted each other warmly: Francis and Susan Higgins. Francis and I with other friends had wandered through Skye and the Outer Isles one autumn while he still lived in Leeds. A gardener, he had been delighted to move to Langwell. I was not absolutely sure if they were there still and my next intention was to knock on a door and ask. The first house was their's anyway.

That really ended the trip, with a bit of a bang, for I was suddenly being fed and spoilt, sleep tonight in a bed and will be borne off to Lochinver by Francis tomorrow to retrieve my car.

However, before anything else, I insisted Storm and I *walked* down to the sea at Berriedale. The crossing of the A9 at the foot of those thundering braes was the most dangerous moment of the crossing! An old castle perched on a cliff noisy with kittiwakes and the sea beyond sparkled cheerily. A sentence from Edward Whymper can sum-up the hike:

"Toil he must who goes mountaineering; but out of the toil comes strength (not merely muscular energy, more than that), an awakening of all the faculties; and from the strength comes pleasure."

15. Pictures from an Expedition
(Tay to Clyde)

IN April 1982 I made a solitary walk across the waist of Scotland, linking the River Tay and the River Clyde along the Ochils, Campsies and Kilpatrick Hills. It was a long-standing idea which followed several ideals.

The Tay-Clyde expedition was to be in the old style: done for fun and interest, nosing out historical associations, re-visiting the known and exploring the new. It was a case of packing a rucksack and going. There was no guide book to follow, no statutory "Way". It was a route for a goat rather than a sheep.

A couple of buses took me across Fife one Thursday near the end of the month. A performance of *Jamie the Saxt* the night before had aroused the historical enthusiasms so it was apt to be starting from Abernethy.

Abernethy was an ancient Pictish capital, had been a great Celtic church centre (it has one of Scotland's two surviving Round Towers) had Roman occupation (with fort, baths and harbour at Carpow), and was linked by ferry to Scone just ten miles to the north, but few areas of rich history have so little to show for it. Abernethy is simply a quiet village now, a dormitory for St John's Town of Perth.

I passed derelict mills and a forgotten quarry before following a woody glen up to the windy crest of the eastern Ochils. The cultivation laps up like waves on a skerry but does not quite sweep over the top. Cool pine forests and moorland with quiet roads led me on. I read a book as I walked. Usually I keep to fiction. Mixing places can have some weird effects to a world-wanderer. Once or twice I have woken from dreams and lain in my tent utterly baffled as to where I was!

There was one delectable rest by an overgrown pond where the moorhens were fussing about like ministers at a General Assembly.

I joined the Glentarkie road, which gives as fine a view as the Lowlands can produce with the brown-breasted serge of ploughed fields and the green shawl of winter sowing leading the eye out over Fife and Kinross to the Lomonds: a lion-couchant shape visible from Soutra on the English border to the ski slopes of Glen Shee. Rarely is the finest landscape empty of man's handiwork. Suilven may stun but it is the little hills that steal the heart away.

The route led on by Beins Law and Pittuncarty and Balvaird (a rose-red tower being restored) to cut through by Corrinzion (which sounds like a Cornich name), Balcanquhal (pronounce that if you can) to reach Glenfarg village by a footbridge over the M90.

After toiling up out of the noisy glen I lunched in the lee on a dyke for the wind was snell. It was cold enough to wear my windproof jacket yet the sun, playing hide-and-seek with cotton wool clouds, was to bronze my brow that day. I left the Path of Condie road, like Glenfarg an historic route to Strathearn and Perth, (which sounds as if Tolkien had been through) and for the rest of the day tracked over bleak moors full of sheep.

It clouded and tried to rain. Instead there was a confetti of snow. Somewhere in the middle of nowhere the tent was pitched. Young trees hardly gave it shelter. The light ran down a scale of tones into night but like a lingering chord there was a breathy brightness right through the dark. The frost fell from the stars to whiten the ground and rime the tent.

A wash of yellow sun over the hills encouraged an early start. Innerdouny was the highest of the eastern Ochils and from it, peering through wind-watering eyes, I could see Ben Vorlich and Stuc a' Chroin sticking up like white teeth.

The Highland Line had been whitewashed by snow overnight. The wind was icy. With gangrel-freedom I gave up plans to camp on Ben Cleuch that night. I would walk along the face of the Ochil scarp instead of over them and today could slitter through to camp at Paradise.

By fell and forest I switchbacked to the Borland Glen to join the old track to Glendevon from Auchterarder. A hail shower made me dive behind a dyke, a shelter shared by a very dead sheep.

Glendevon in the sunshine was delightful. So full of memories, too. Growing up in Dollar it marked the natural bounds of our wanderings afoot and by bike. We had watched the youth hostel being built. On Sabbath rangings we would drop in to the clean-lined little church (with its huge manse) with our boots and rucksacks. We had cantered over on horseback through Glenquey. We had

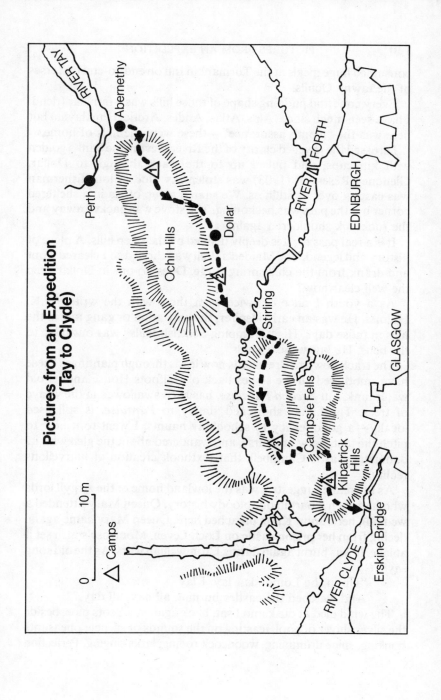

Pictures from an Expedition
(Tay to Clyde)

RIVER TAY

Perth

Abernethy

Ochil Hills

Dollar

Stirling

RIVER FORTH

EDINBURGH

Campsie Fells

GLASGOW

Kilpatrick Hills

Erskine Bridge

RIVER CLYDE

△ Camps

10 m

0

consumed huge meals at the Tormankin Inn on end-to-end traverses of the tawny Ochils.

Every cone and pudding shape of those hills was a familiar friend. I have seen much since (Alps, Atlas, Andes, Arctic, Himalayas) but here was the "womb assurance"—these were the hills of home.

I crossed the jewelled clarity of the River Devon, the banks golden with kingcups, and pulled up to the track through to Dollar, Glenquey Reservoir (1903) was stolen-sky blue. A lone fisherman was casting over its stillness. We shared a cup of tea in a sheltered corner but the pass was beckoning. The stove was packed away and the rucksack shouldered again.

It is a real pass for it is deeply defined by the steep hills. A place of history and legend. The Maiden's Well was choked so I cleared it out and drank from the chill spring surge. Does no-one in Dollar keep the well clear now?

As a youth I once or twice went there with the writer W.K. Holmes. He was an early inspirer, the only adult or gang met in the hills in those days. His "Tramping Scottish Hills" was our bible to the bens. He knew the legends.

The track down to Brewlands now leads through plantings. These have smothered all the slopes back o' Hillfoots House and its old water tank, our *Second Paradise,* has been swallowed in the weave of trees. The name, shortened simply to *Paradise,* is still used locally—a good legacy to schoolday haunts. I went to it now to pitch the tent, brew of course, and wandered about the glen with its dominant Castle Campbell, that textbook creation of marvellous reality.

As the name suggests it was the lowland home of the Argyll lords who had such a part in our bloody history. Queen Mary attended a wedding here. John Knox preached here. Queen Mary came again, fleeing from her prison castle on Loch Leven. Montrose's men set it ablaze. It was burnt again during Cromwellian wars. As the old song says:

> "Up in the Lomonds I lay, I lay,
> And watched the castles burning all day, all day."

The wind died at dusk and I sat, back against a Scots pine, beside the silver shiver of pool, feasting on the sounds of silence: pheasants honking, snipe drumming, woodcock roding, larks singing. Perfection occasionally comes to mortals in the quiet places of the spirit.

"The Hillfoots" is the historical if ungrammatical term for the villages snuggling under the steep front of the Ochils: Dollar, Tillicoultry, Alva, Menstrie... The day's walk kept me moving westwards above them, sometimes on made routes, sometimes on mere sheep tracks.

My main memory is of trees. Above Harviestoun or between Tilly and Alva there were some colossal pines, beech, sycamore, yews and other exotics from the days of Victorian estates. They were full of rabbits and roe deer which came close to the silent watcher, passed, then would wind me and tear away in a riot of leaves.

It became one of the hottest days of the year and maybe I was lucky in abandoning walking for the day at Alva. A business meeting held me there from lunch to tea and I lingered with friends for supper and then it was dark before I reached Dumyat and the planned camp on the Inchna Burn. In the gloaming I just found a trickle of a stream amoung the whins and set up the tent in its dewy dell.

Blairlogie is worth walking across Scotland to see. Parts of the charming village are of great age—something our history has usually destroyed. I passed through it in the early morning with not a soul to be seen. It was almost spooky.

Like all travellers of old I perforce crossed the Forth at Stirling, by that ancient bridge of grace and strength, watched over by the Wallace Monument on one side and Stirling Castle on the other. Sheriffmuir lay to the north, Bannockburn to the south. Cambuskenneth occupies a link in the Forth downstream.

You can hardly avoid history here and the classroom phrase "lowest bridging point" takes sudden life. If any town should stir the blood, it is Stirling. Wander up by the Castle and you could be back in the seventeenth century. Even the youth hostel building is of that vintage. It was all quiet and deserted at seven o'clock on a Sunday morning.

Canoeing down the Forth from Loch Ard had already brought home to me the "gateway" character of Stirling. Anciently Flanders Moss had been like a moat holding back the wild north. Travellers and fugitives, business and commerce, raiders and armies all had to break through at Stirling. Only the Rob Roys of this world knew the secrets of passing the moss otherwise. I headed up to the co-barrier of hills: Touch Hills, Gargunnock Hills, Fintry Hills, Campsies.

The latter name is often used for all of them, and invariably raises village patriotism in vigorous protest. I think they ended with such a proliferation of names because, anciently, they were only known and used peripherally from those places. They are an elevated Flanders Moss, a geographical wilderness which deflected all to Stirling. The long cliff-edged skyline had always attracted me. Now I would walk it.

From Cambusbarron pleasant farm tracks led up into the Touch Hills. The vivid green fields were buttoned with sheep. The plain was hazy, heat-exhausted, the Ochils a blue rampart. In a mini-gorge wall-papered with primroses I had a long break. On a big walking tour many of the most memorable places are brew stops.

The next two miles to Carleatheran, overlooking Gargunnock, probably gave four miles of actual walking. It was bog and heather with all kinds of frustrating ingredients added. Real steamed pudding textures. The descent beyond was easier but a visit to the Spout of Ballochleam disappointed. The long drought had reduced the Boquhan Burn to a tepid trickle. I followed it up to the dazzle of westings and very near the top of Stronend, 1,677 feet, highest of the Fintry Hills, made camp—the one really high overnight stop.

Descending to Fintry gave some interesting moments. An overnight "haar" hid the western tiers of cliff and picking a way down them, unseen, from above required some care. On the lower slopes a jungly stream led me down into Culcreuch grounds and I exited by a drive which was marked PRIVATE. How lush and colourful the Endrick Valley seemed after the wastelands above.

Fintry is a neat little place. The friendly shop provided fresh rolls and fruit for a second breakfast in a beech wood quivering with cool yellow sunlight. It was back to the oven after that, up by Dunmore, a prehistoric fort, and site of a Covenanting skirmish in 1679, finally to gain Earl's Seat 1,896 feet, highest point of the whole walk. There are some spectacular corries to the north, curved round in almost regular arcs by the Great Mathematician in the sky.

The going was easier: crackly burnt moorland or dried peat bogs, seamed and lined like age. Suddenly the ground fell away again in steep grass slopes to the Blane valley, a plaid of cultivation,

The Loup o' Fintry in the Campsie Fells

with a series of odd paps slipping out to remind of the harsh past. Prehistoric fort sites, standing stones, a medieval castle milestoned our way.

The most remarkable of all the bumps is Dumgoyne. What should be a ridge dropping down to the valley suddenly changes its mind and climbs up into a knobble several hundreds of feet high, right in the western extremity of the miles of flat moorland. Some youngsters were making a rush-and-rest sort of assault on it as I left. What a contrast to come down through fields of lambs and fussy pheasants on to the A81. The commuters were tearing home.

I found myself on the West Highland Way but it was obviously signposted for those going north. I chose the shadiest of four possible tracks and in that last sizzle of tea-time sun paused by some standing stones to admire Dumgoyne again.

A pub at Carbeth was welcome and after a half-mile of tar I headed for the wilds again. One moment I was watching some wild slicing of balls into the Allander Water on Craigton Golf Course, the next I was on curlew-crying moors. When the sun heat turned down I pitched and ate lazily by a friendly burn.

These Kilpatrick Hills have a strange bumpy heartland which has made the building of reservoirs simple. There must be a dozen or so. My route linked Black Loch; Cochno Loch; Greenside and Burnbrae Reservoirs. The first was high and dark enough. The second had an island in the middle linked by two causeways which could have been a setting for a Henty yarn of Cortez's attack on the Mexico City of the Aztecs.

I crossed it and turned a hill to the third. The Clyde still was hidden, so I skirted round and down to Burnbrae. Still no view down to the salty waters. The exit stream suddenly pitched over on to a "den" and from the lip I was suddenly looking down on the great curve of the Erskine Bridge. This new lowest bridging point would be a good finish. I crossed the line of Antonine's Wall just before going underground in the convolutions of approach roads. The commuters this time were all roaring into the city.

We joined them, travelling in by train and then home for teatime. There is nothing like BR to bring civilisation back to the wanderer. The train to Edinburgh was late so I missed my connection for Fife, the heaters were full on, there was no water in the toilet—yet people thought I had been "roughing it".

Scotland's beauty is her wilderness, but we seem hell-bent on making her just like anywhere else. This trip was simply a personal reaffirmation of our freedom to roam. As such it had no real ending. It can be picked up any time, extended, diverted.

This Tay-Clyde jaunt had stopped on Monday. The following weekend saw my dog Storm and I homeward bound from Loch Fyne with a diversion to Fintry and Kippen for a performance of Faure's *Requiem*. It was the second of May. The windscreen wipers were on double speed and fighting not to clog up with snow. The hills were invisible. Being Sunday Clucreuch Castle was open so we drove up to it for some tea. (It is a traditional tower rather overwhelmed with later additions).

The driveway was a rushing torrent and the sheep in the fields looked pathetic. One lamb was perched on its mother's back to avoid the flooded grass. The castle, seen through the snow, looked very like a Christmas-card picture. We left by the drive on to which I had descended from Stronend; that double scarp now loomed out of the breaking cloud, black as liquorice layered with sugary white snow bands.

We drove up the Endrick Valley to see the Loup of Fintry, surely one of the land's finest waterfalls, yet unmarked on the Ordnance Survey map. It was a brown cataract, leaping and spreading over several ledges and sending the spray high out of the woody gorge that hides it so well from the casual motorist. This was a day for waterfalls, not summits.

A mile on past where the Endrick swings down out of the hills we reached the Carron Valley Reservoir. The Endrick waters flow to the Clyde, the Carron's to the Forth. Such a watershed was the natural place to cook supper before going off for the Endrick Singers' Performance. This brief meteorological tantrum was the odd highlight of the Tay-Clyde journey. The sting in the tail. The end of this tale.

"FURTH" OF SCOTLAND

Unfairly I think I am often cast as the fervent Scottish nationalist. In reality I spend a great deal of time out of Scotland, including wandering the hills of England, Wales and Ireland, which are all excellent in their ways. It does the bottom-heavy end of England no harm however to realise that Britain includes other countries and outlooks which are as valid as their own. Writing in magazines I am constantly trying to interpret Scotland's traditions (they are so easily swamped) but in these pieces I am basically doing the opposite—telling Scotsman *readers of the good things elsewhere in Britain. Insularity and ignorance are not the sins of the south-east of England only! If I am biased towards the Scottish landscape this is hardly surprising and it is a view shared south of the Border judging by the armies of walkers and climbers which invade whenever holidays come along. I mean to say would* you *rather spend the weekend on the hills of Kent or on the hills of Torridon?*

16. Furth: The Lakeland Fells

MY first recorded "Munro" was Ben Nevis, then 4,406 feet, the highest summit in the British Isles and an ambitious attitude to a solitary wandering lad more used to the grassy Ochils.

It was climbed in thick mist, spurred on by W.K. Holmes' book "Tramping Scottish Hills," which spoke of a breathtaking, ever-widening view as one gained height up its desolate shoulders. I am affraid my annotations in the margin were cynical!

It was bitter cold, even in mid-August, the wetness of my legs turned to ice by the summit cairn. I was still to learn that the mean temperature is one degree below freezing, that only about one day in ten will give a view (which can be magnificent, especially in the evening) and that given two or three extra hundred feet there would be a permanent ice cap on top.

I have reached the summit since then by scores of routes, up classic rock-routes, some of the longest in Britain, up icy gullies, up in visibility that masked more than a few feet ahead, up to arrive soaked through, up on hands and knees unable to stand against the wind, up to lie by the cairn in sunshine under skies blue-deep as Mont Blanc's.

Typically, it has given the varied experience that mountaineering offers in Scotland. It *can* be walked up with no more danger than Arthur's Seat on a warm June dusk. It *can* be as difficult and desperate a summit to reach as any in the Alps.

After Ben Nevis I launched out onto further hills, usually using "bike and hike" usually staying in Youth Hostels, then only 1/6d. a night for a youngster, usually buying tins of war surplus day rations. How much the modern teenager has missed in some things.

Several years must have passed before I knew what a "Munro" was or its difference from a "Top". After that, though, they were carefully noted, not however to the extent of becoming a "mere Munro-bagger", equal joy could be found in lower hills in Arran or Sutherland or my own Ochils.

Fifteen years after that solitary climb up Ben Nevis the last of the Munros and Tops was climbed. The last Munro was again kept as a solo effort: Sgurr na Ciche on the edge of the rough Bounds of Knoydart, climbed from a bothy one Hogmanay, a week before setting off for a winter's mountaineering in Morocco.

Back from the edge of the Sahara the last Tops, on Beinn Eighe, were climbed during a weekend with three youngsters from Braehead School where I taught. It took three trains, six buses, seven lifts and much walking for the five glorious hours on that Torridon Ridge. Perhaps the modern affluent teenager is not so different after all!

Thirty years of wandering in other lands, other ranges, has only deepened this first love; but it is still interesting—and perhaps essential to visit other places. So, long before completing Scotland's Munros and Tops, I had already gone "Furth of Scotland" to climb and explore.

That term, however, has a special connotation to British climbers. Munros are purely Scottish things, the name coming from Sir Hugh Munro who first listed (and very nearly climbed) them in leisurely Victorian days.

"Furth of Scotland" was the delicately, diplomatic phrase coined by Eric Maxwell, the recorder of these collections, for those bumps rising above the 3,000 ft mark "abroad," "south of the border"— England with 7, Wales 14 and Ireland 13. (This is taking in separate mountains *and* subsidiary bumps—the Munros and Tops equivalent.)

Perhaps it is a good thing to have this additional challenge, a continuing motive for braving rain and snow, floods and midges, even heatwaves. It certainly is a challenge to "logistics", distances, costs, times, sleeping quarters, transport are all suddenly more important.

When school closed at four on a Friday afternoon, we were usually in Inverness for chip suppers by eight, which virtually places anywhere in Scotland within range of weekend motorised climbing. It was a surprise to find this could apply as easily to the Lake District and almost to Wales.

My brief visits Furth of Scotland have been enough to form certain impressions, to revel in the differences and rejoice in the similarities, to find some places dull, while of others we cried: "We'll take that back with us!"

It was only at the last minute when an unexpected Monday holiday came up that I decided to visit the Lakes, too late to rope anyone else in, so it was "me and my dog" who set off in the big Hillman Estate: howff as well as transport. We ran into cold, clear weather that shone the hills in gold each dawn. In Keswick we also ran into Tom Wier. These wandering Scots!

There had been no time to read up on the area, so I simply had a one inch Ordnance Survey map with the vital statistics of heights added. We camped in the car outside Keswick that night no later than if we had camped by Kinlochewe. The roads and valleys, the wooded lakes are all very neat and clean . . . at the price of restrictive "no parking," "no camping," "no road" signs.

We drove through charming scenery to Seathwaite where there were still signs of floods: fences broken and debris-covered, foundations of buildings laid bare and tide-marks up the walls.

At the head of the valley we scrambled up a gully onto "Big End". From there we went over Scafell Pike, at 3,210 ft, England's highest, then scrambled up Scafell from Mickledore. Deep Ghyll, a traverse

Castlerigg Stone Cirles above Keswick with Skiddaw behind

to Styhead and round and up Great Gable led to a sunset view down to the green patchwork of Wasdale.

On the way, unexpectedly, I met crags that were instantly known from photographs. There was the frightful East Buttress of Scafell, the classic Flake Crank on Central Buttress, Kern Knotts Crack, Nape's Needle. This was where climbing history, south of the Border, began. Almost hallowed ground, like St Kilda where climbing goes back hundreds of years. From the top of Scafell Pike the coast was silver and grey: sea and smoke; a power station sticking up as stark and ugly as the Aviemore Centre from the Cairngorms.

We woke to a fog that lay coldly on the valley, but after inching through Keswick to gain a few hundred feet we broke out into a blaze of autumn bracken on golden slopes. Skiddaw, steep but cragless, is a walker's hill. Kitchy ran daft in the dawn light: slowly the smoky rooftops of Keswick broke through the clouds and Derwentwater danced with reflections. We were "loath to come down" that testimony of content. It was the last day of October. The beeches had spread carpets of bronze along Ullswater. Already flecks of snow lay on the peaks.

Helvellyn was traversed by the historic Striding Edge ("Hey, moom, thar's dog doing t'Edge"); perhaps disappointing as thirty people crowded it while another thirty roamed the summit. What must it be like in busy summer? It is, of course, the viewpoint looking over the twenty eight square miles of Cumberland and Westmorland (= Cumbria) forming "The Lake District." (As in Scotland there is really only one *lake*. The rest are 'waters' or 'tarns'.)

I could have been home with my "bag" that evening, but drove instead to Langdale from Windermere. It was quite shockingly busy, every rock seemed to have a rope on it, every nook a picnic party, but I met possibly the finest surprise of the trip, the road over the Wrynose and Hard Knot Passes. The Bealach nam Bo is nothing to this motorists' thrill! We stopped on top for the night, the sun like a squashed raspberry where grey sea met grey sky.

Monday took us up Wasdale for a deluge on Pillar, so we were down before Wasdale Head had cleared breakfast. Home! The Lakes love had commenced. The books of Harry Griffin are a good introduction to Lakeland Fells. "Long Days in the Hills" is perhaps my favourite.

Furth: The Ridges of Snowdon

If you only like uncrowded mountains, do not go to Snowdon. When I wandered round the justly famous Snowdon Horseshoe at the end of June I estimated that I saw or met about six hundred other people—and that was not counting the hundreds going up and down by the railway. Somehow, the summit of Wales survives.

Because I like quiet, uncrowded mountains, my visits to Snowdon have usually had some special motivation. The first time was simply to help complete all the 3,000 foot summits "Furth of Scotland." The second visit was to allow my dog Kitchy and the pupils from Braehead School to complete their respective Munros. The next visit was a soaking along Crib Goch and then it was climbed twice during the Groats End Walk, where we linked the four country summits on foot. Even with those four routes on two days we had not exhausted the mountain.

For once, Crib Goch had not been included. It is Wales's counterpart to the Aonach Eagach in Glencoe. It was back in June, at long last, we went right round the whole horseshoe. Some day when we are wealthy enough we might even go up in the train!

The day we took the school kids up was one of thick mist and, after groping along Crib Goch, I told them to be careful or they might get run over by a train. I was given some rude looks, but a few minutes later there was a pulsing beat, growing ever-louder, and slowly the looks became those of complete surprise as, out of the mist, came a train. The railway is quite an asset to navigation under those circumstances; you just follow the line. It is narrow guage and with a rack in the middle. With its summit station at 3,500 feet it is just over four and a half miles in length. Swiss locomotives do the work.

A recent innovation with public transport has been the creation of a round-Snowdonia bus shuttle, so you can cut clear of your car for a day (or more) and also have complete freedom to go up and down by different routes and be sure of transport back. The peak is surrounded by youth hostels and huts and famous old inns and hamlets. Snowdonia is organised all right. The Welsh don't miss much and though they may chat away in their own tongue and spray road signs that appear in English, there seems to be no translation for Bed and Breakfast.

Before Telford took his A5 road through Snowdonia to Holyhead, and there was only a track up Llanberis, the region must have been one of stark, grand scenery—very much "Wild Wales." It was the slate-quarrying as much as anything that opened it up; the great block of mountains was, like Gaul, divided into three parts.

Nearest to Scotland and moated by sea on west and north is the Carneddau, vast, grassy uplands with semi-wild ponies chasing the winds. South, across the Nant Ffrancon/Capel Curig (A5) road lie the Glydders range: hills deeply bitten into by cwms and leaving shattered ridges and peaks like Tryfan, which is worth a Geal Charn or two. South again over the Glen Ogle-like Pass of Llanberis is Snowdon itself—no more a single peak than Beinn Eighe or Cruachan, but where they are just skirted by road, Snowdon is surrounded. In some ways it is a single peak, for Yr Wyddfa dominates and is centrally placed like the hub of a wheel—a Catharine Wheel, perhaps, for ridges seem to fly off in all directions.

There are six major ridges and between them dark lochans and some big cliffs, including "Cloggy." Two of these ridges circle eastwards to form the classic horseshoe. There are at least six main ascent routes, worn into vivid erosion scars by the thousands of tramping feet, and leaflets and guide books galore describe every tiny detail.

I stayed at the Pen-y-Pass youth hostel, very much a walkers' and climbers' centre as it long has been. I set off up the path which, like all the others, is being made into a "proper" one to try to curtail the erosion. I was nearly blown off it by a helicopter on exercise and later on I nearly jumped off it as two jets screamed past, *below* me, down Llanberis Pass. I passed about a score of people and on the top found another score and on the rooftop leading to the pinnacles I bypassed another score, all in identical garb.

Crib Goch is the "interesting" way up Snowdon, but it is not really the route for the large school parties. It is exposed and any slip could well be fatal. When the alternative to staying on is falling off it is surprising how few choose the latter course! There is a knife-edge ridge to start and then a series of jagged pinnacles. It was along this ridge that we had our Snowdon introduction one winter and were caught in a storm. Two fellow teachers (female) and a student friend.

It was quite an epic and by the time we had cleared all the difficulties and were wandering up to the summit our four had grown to fourteen as various gangs tagged on.

On the way down I have a vivid picture of one of the girls, no lightweight, lying with her ice axe hooked over the railway line to stop being blown away. Later, we found a party in trouble and had to call out a rescue. Another abiding memory of that day is of "lunching" in the lee of the summit station. It was simply a case of cramming in calories and the mixture of spindrift, pineapple chunks and sardines is not one that I would recommend. Our water bottles had frozen solid. Memorable of course.

Once we reached the line of the railway this time it was as busy as Princes Street in mid-December. It was almost a case of queuing for the cairn. Just spitting distance down from the summit is the top station and a pub-cum-cafe. There is no escaping the queue there! Descending on the Lliwedd side, I had to fight a tide of more than fifty kids in one group and Lliwedd, which should habe been quiet, was circled for twenty minutes by a helicopter which only went away when we started throwing stones at it!

After that though, I had the mountains to myself. It was tea time. We lay on the end peak above Cwm Dyli till the sun shivered off and a cloud formed over the summit of Wales. Munroist or not, do make the effort of exploring Snowdon and the other 3,000ders. The fourteen summits in a go is a popular challenge and it and other stories are well told in the Thomas Firbanks book "Give Me This Mountain." Poucher, Styles, Rowlands and Terry Marsh amongst others have written guides to all the Snowdon 3,000ders.

Furth: The Quiet Hills of Ireland

I have always been interested in the way language changes and words alter their meaning. But I'm not so sure about the changing use of the word Munro.

Sir Hugh Munro of Lindertis was a well-to-do Victorian gentleman with many interests and talents, including an enthusiasm for his own Scottish hills which he explored long before roads and railways made it the easy game it is today!

It was not even known how many hills of stature there were in the country. Only recently had Ben Nevis been clearly shown to be higher than Macdhui. So, when his Tables of Mountains over 3,000 feet appeared in the 1891 Scottish Mountaineering Club Journal, it caused wide interest.

It was not long before the term Munro was applied to these summits above the magic plimsol line. Sir Hugh died in the First World War with two Munros unclimbed and it was left to the Rev. A.E. Robertson in 1901 to pass that historic milestone.

Only eight people had done the Munros prior to the Second World War (three are still alive, so it is obviously a healthy activity), but now it has become a very popular game indeed. Only about one in ten go on to complete the 3,000 foot hills "Furth of Scotland." South of the Border they are now tending to appropriate yet another institution by talking of English Munros. Is nothing sacred?

Not inappropriately, its first blatant use was by an Englishman writing a guide book to the "Irish Munros." He has now compounded the felony with "Welsh Munros" and "English Munros." The word is beyond saving, I fear.

Harry Mulholland is to be congratulated on producing very useful guides and the Irish one was particularly welcome as there had been a dearth of information about those splendid hills. The Irish maps alone are anything but an aid to finding summits.

In Scotland, we only count the distinctive summits as Munros, other bumps over 3,000 feet being subsidiary "Tops." England follows suit, claiming four summits over the height (with three subsidiary bumps) but the Welsh try to boost things with a claim to 14 "Threes," which is really only eight Munros and six tops. Ireland has never been sure just what is what, but as Brandon, Galteemore and the Lug are all solitary summits, it is only in the Reeks that happy chaos is maintained and there a complete traverse of everything is such an enjoyable outing that a big day is welcomed. It is worth saving for a clear day. With only thirty four Bumps and Bunions Furth of Scotland you can afford to mac siccar.

If I've gone into that at length it is because I am always being asked about it. It must be a British trait to take our sports and pastimes so seriously while serious things like politics are a cause of humour.

I think I enjoy climbing and walking in Ireland, now, because it

Legananny Dolmen with the Mountains of Mourne on the skyline

reminds me of my own youthful first wanderings in the wilds. Ireland is not organised, it is not over-run by belisha-bright mobs, its maps are laughable, its ungraded youth hostels full of character, its people (mountainy or otherwise) are marvellously friendly and the landscape positively bursts with antiquities—and, for sure, it has some good mountains.

Much of this comes as a surprise to walkers who may know England, Scotland and Wales well enough. Perhaps there had been a dearth of written comment and description but several "greats" such as Norman Collie and Geoffrey Winthrop Young knew and loved the Irish hills. The latter's poem *Brandon Bay* could have been written yesterday so little has the scene changed. (It is in the anthology "Speak to the Hills".)

This unhurried feeling of the past is one of the attractions of Ireland. You have to go to Shetland or the Outer Hebrides to find it elsewhere. Not much has changed in hundreds of years: electricity may have come and the donkeys gone and there are comfy new houses but the people are still on the land and the crofts are still lived on, right into the heart of the mountains.

I set great store on character. After all our physical act of climbing or walking does not change really whether done in Patterdale or Patagonia. The differences hold the secret of delight—and Ireland is rich enough in character for six nations. As a Scot with roots in the west there is the tremendous Gaelic cultural link. One Gaelic can be understood by the others (map names are familiar), we share the same folklore, we have suffered a like history summed up in two words: the English.

I had not realised just how biased history was until I found it comically embarrassing while leading walking gangs in Ireland, to be constantly saying of a ruin "It was destroyed by Cromwell" or of a city, "The English did this or other". In Scotland I know my schooling mentioned nothing of the Clearances—which directly make the Highlands what they are now scenically. I would even suggest, as I've done before, that Ireland has the edge on Scotland scenically because her countryside is still lived in. On the remotest hill you may suddenly catch a whiff of a turf (peat) reek.

I usually escape to Ireland every other Autumn. Most trips have taken in Ireland's 3000 ft mountains, for there will always be one or two Munro-baggers amoung us keen to add the English, Welsh and Irish ones to a growing or completed Scottish tally.

Because they are well placed and so different from the sterile home hostels we usually use *An Oige* youth hostels. Foulksrath is a fourteenth century keep (*not* destroyed by the English), Loo Bridge is a converted railway station, Killary Harbour has a gable in the sea and curraghs at the door. We have also used a caravan looking out on a four-mile strand on the Dingle peninsula, a climbers' inn in Kerry, or we have camped or stayed in bed and breakfast—all unbooked for, wanting to see as much as possible and walk as many hills as possible, movements could not be planned. It would be easiest, perhaps, to make a typical two week "tour" on paper here to give ideas and inspiration to tempt you west over sea.

Our first week usually concentrates on Ireland's 3,000ders, just in case the fickle weather, petrol strikes or other acts of God or man conspire to foil the sufferers of this weird mania. The meeting point is the Saturday evening ferry from Holyhead from which we drive up to Knockree YH in the Wicklow Mountains.

The Wicklows run south from Dublin in great peaty domes which in places can make Kinder look a garden. The highest is Lugnaquillia and, being weekend, near the capital you may actually meet others on the hill. Frequently on our tours this has proved the only encounter with other walkers in the two weeks.

Glendalough, an old monastic site, is our first call and the first Round Tower is seen there. These have the appeal of brochs at home, being equally unique in one period and place. By some people traversing and others (usually me, wanting other hills) going round, longer days on the tops can be made here and elsewhere. If it is a miserable day it can be romped and the comforts of Ballinclea YH sought out.

We usually have an "off" day thereafter as there is just so much of interest to see in motoring west: Kilkenny, Cahir Castle, the Rock of Cashel, old abbeys, Round Towers, river scenery and so on—and a night at Foulksrath Castle. Weeding the moat is one of the odder duties I've been asked to do.

The Galtymore hills provide another 3,000der and whether this is done alone or in some combination or a long traverse we usually end in Ballydavid Wood YH. It is an old farmhouse with a huge oak tree beside it. Years ago the old warden told me a famous historian had worked under its shade. The way she spoke it sounded recent but Fr Keating lived in the seventeenth century!

Galtymore and its brother hills rise boldly out of the incredibly green farmscape which here and there has donned the rougher serge of vast forestry plantings. They give a superb long traverse which I've described in the "Groats End Walk" book.

The Knockmealdowns and Comeragh Mountains, south of the Galtrees, or a whole succession of hills in West Cork or Kerry beg for some of the next day. If pushed the Reeks could be nibbled at then but they deserve a full day untouched by motoring. C.W. Wall's "Mountaineering in Ireland" (FMCI Guide) is the equivalent of Munro's, or Bridge's Tables, and lists all the Irish 2,000 foot hills. There are plenty of them! It is probably worth ending at Carrauntoohil Y.H., an old schoolhouse, to the north of the Macgillycuddy Reeks for I think the easiest traverse of all the 3,000-ers can be made from there if you are required to return to a car. The map outlines this.

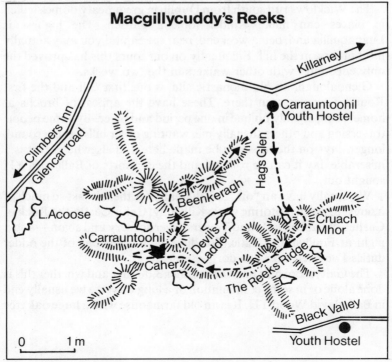

Macgillycuddy's Reeks

Killarney →

Carrauntoohil
Youth Hostel

Climbers Inn

Glencar road

Hag's Glen

Beenkeragh

L.Acoose

Cruach
Mhor

Carrauntoohil

Devil's
Ladder

Caher

The Reeks Ridge

Black Valley

0   1 m

Youth Hostel

The Reeks would appear in any "top ten" list of British and Irish big ridges. Comparisons are difficult, if not odious, but there is something of the Mamores in the Reeks plus maybe a bit of Torridon—for on a couple of places there is exposed scrambling. From the YH gentle walking leads to brutal steepness to gain Cruach Mhor, the most easterly peak. A shrine-cairn makes it unmistakable even in thick mist. From there the first two sweeping dips give some of the exciting narrowness but the way is becoming increasingly tracked with use.

The rest of the Reeks proper are a mossy carpet which is all too apt to fly from under one on the downhills. The lowest point is joined by the "tourist route" just before Carrauntoohil but, ignore it briefly, to slope out for the Caher tops westwards, then make the full circuit of the highest and Beenkeragh: a magnificent lough-held corrie. Between Carrauntoohil and Beenkeragh there is some good scrambling. In places old fossil ripple marks can be seen in the red sandstone that caps every 3,000 foot summit in Ireland.

From Beenkeragh a steep, rough descent can be made back to the hostel. This outline can be used in conjunction with the guides mentioned for I think they often miss the point of the having to return to a starting point.

At Glencar, west of the Reeks, The Climbers' Inn is another possible base. Brandon could even be done from there though away out on a peninsula. There is a desperate need for an official Youth Hostel in Dingle though one has recently opened at Dunquin and Dingle does have a couple of private hostels and camping fields. I can recommend the hotel at Cloghane if climbing Brandon from that side.

Brandon is worth keeping to the last. The western side of it is plain grassiness up which wanders a "Saint's Road," a route pioneered by St Brendan, the Navigator, who built an oratory on top, founded various religious houses, visited St Kilda and possibly even America. (Read Tim Severin's "The Brendan Voyage").

The eastern side is a shocking contrast, of Torridonian grandeur: a series of silver loughs set in deeper and deeper hollows and overlooked by black prows of rock. A route up the lochs or by the Pilgrim path from Cloghane and Faha are sure to yield great days. Being the nearest hill to America however Brandon can be woefully wet. The week may be needed, and even the second one, to climb all the threes in reasonable conditions.

Assuming a week has seen the Munros accomplished our gangs tend either to turn back for the endless options in Kerry or we wander up to Connemara and back by the Boyne Valley where the prehistoric site of Newgrange is one of the world's wonders. The southern route can take in Blarney Castle—at which spot I should perhaps stop, not, I hope, without stirring up some desire, "some day", to take your boots across to these forgotten hills. They should be an unforgettable memory.

17. Ben Nevis—Weather on not

THE rock-climbing guide to Ben Nevis has this phrase in it: "Altitude and proximity to the western seaboard expose Ben Nevis to weather conditions probably unique in Europe."

The altitude is that of being Tops in Britain and were it only about 300 feet higher, we would have a real glacier permanently on this 4406-foot giant. It went up to 4418 ft just before metrification; the re-surveying also pushed 3999 ft. Aonach Mor over the 4000 ft level, making eight of those, split between Lochaber and the Cairngorms.

The uniqueness of the weather is largely connected with cloud and rain. You have only one chance in ten of having it clear on the summit, according to statistics. Of course it can be clear for weeks at a time but, alas, is all too true normally. Look at some of the findings from the years the Observatory was operating on the summit (1884-1901). The mean temperature over those 17 years was 31.4 deg. F— below freezing point! One year gave 240 inches of rain.

It is almost impossible to imagine what life must have been like a hundred years ago, with trains just penetrating to the north, Munro's Tables just published, no slick gear, no youth hostels, and no cars—all the things which make our hill going so easy. Compare our doings with a weekend had by Tough and Brown, who set off from Edinburgh to climb the North-East Buttress in May 1895.

They took the overnight train to Kingussie and set off on push bikes at 3.50 a.m. Two hours later they had a puncture—the bang sounding "like the opening of six bottles of Bouvier"—so they had to walk three miles to Laggan Inn, hoping for a horse and trap there. There was no transport, so they took turns with the one gear-laden bike for a further thirteen miles to Tulloch Station where a train got them to Fort William by noon. An hour later they set off for the Allt a' Mhuillin. The hills were blotted out in cloud and a cloudburst did not help. It was 6.15 p.m. before they roped up for what is still a long, demanding route.

They escaped into the gloaming at the back of ten and after being entertained by the Observatory staff and having forty winks were back in the Fort to catch the 4 a.m. mail-gig to Kingussie, then the train home to Edinburgh, a round trip of 45 hours. They thought they had bagged a fine new route, only for the next Alpine Journal to casually mention an ascent by the Hopkinson brothers three years earlier!

There is a vastly entertaining old book about the Observatory which has recently been reprinted. "Twenty Years on Ben Nevis" (W.T. Kilgour) is a chatty account of life spent on top of the Ben and has some fascinating illustrations of the Observatory buildings covered in fog crystals, of ping-pong being played on a "table made of a block of ice" and of some very dignified "tobogganing." Sometimes the snow so covered the buildings that they had to build a conning tower entrance twenty feet above ground level to ensure they could get out to carry on their meteorological recordings. In one storm one observer had to sit on the legs of another who was trying to take readings at the door. He did not dare go outside in case he was blown away. When he shoved out the anemometer to see what the speed was, the instrument was simply bent over by the wind.

Everybody seems to have been up the Ben. One unlikely visitor was the poet John Keats, who dutifully wrote some bad verse about it, but far from being the imagined soft poet, Keats and his friend Brown had walked there from Lancaster! They walked over the Western Highlands and Islands, but the Ben overtaxed the poet and soon the ravages of TB proved fatal. "I will climb through the clouds—and exist" has a poignant ring, with hindsight.

I have a soft spot for the Ben as it was my very first Munro and is the one I have been up more than all others, except Cairngorm which hardly counts as that was usually by ski lift to start tours into the wilds. The comparative effort is rather different. Ben Nevis is climbed from sea level. The super athletes nip up and back from Fort William in an hour and a half! Most pedestrians are more than happy to devote a day to the ascent. Climbers have been known to require a bivouac!

My only plea about the Ben is to treat it with care. The summit must be one of the biggest middens in the land, dotted with cairns and endless memorial tablets to man's vanity and imbecility, with the Observatory ruins and all the litter of the visiting hordes. It is sordid rather than incongrous to watch a snow bunting rummaging in a poke of crusts and orange peel.

To anyone except the greenest novices, I would also suggest finding better ways up the Ben than just flogging up the tourist path. There are many possibilities available—even up by the waterslide from the car park as the head of Glen Nevis though the rescue folk have stuck a notice up saying not to go that way, which is an impertinence. It's their job to pick up the bits, not tell us where to go. A notice pointing out the (mild) dangers would be in order. The present wording is not.

One of the great ways up is along the Carn Mor Dearg Arete, that swooping, knife-edged ridge which, though over 4,000 feet, is made to look small by the mighty bulk of the Ben.

There is an old story of the pioneer days about it. An expert was taking a young lad up the Ben, via the Arete, and before setting out had explained how, if the leader was to fall off, the second man had to quickly jump off on the other side so the connecting rope would then balance them safely rather than simply jerk number two off as well. It is an interesting technique to practice. Anyway, this pair arrived safely on top of the Ben. Amid his profuse thanks, the lad said: "Sir, I was ready, had you fallen off one side I would have leapt off the other." The old man shook his head and then observed: "Aye,aye, lad, but yon's a technique you only use when we're employing the rope!"

At one time there was just one dignified plaque on top of the Ben. It read: "BEN NEVIS 4406 feet" and, in the more modest lettering, "Erected by the Scottish Mountaineering Club". Not a bad job at all, lads, not bad at all.

WAYS AND MEANS

Walking is only one means to an end, albeit the primary one and the exloration and understanding of our wild heritage allows many different approaches. The next four pieces tell of escapades by push bike, ski, canoe and sailing ship—an indictive sample. Like walking they are all fairly kind on the landscape itself. Only when pursuits tarnish the environment do they become questionable I feel. I like seeing people doing things requiring a certain initiative—and enjoying their adventurings. With but modest talent (plus the curiosity of a mongoose) even I have relished the rich variety of our heritage! If we want something badly enough we will usually find the ways and means of gaining it.

18. A cycle link

LET me describe one of the more unusual hours of last summer. It was one I consciously savoured for I had come many cycle miles that day, through roadblasting heat, to Keswick.

Plenty of restorative liquid and a good meal were followed by a seat on the balcony of the youth hostel, which projected over the River Greta and was deliciously cool. Across the river a cricket match was being played on the green and high above the trees the evening sun was slowly setting on fire the bulk of Skiddaw. The tranquillity and civilised Englishness of the scene was novel for a Scot's gangrel more used to the wilds and weather of the Minch. Why was I cycling such places?

In "Hamish's Groats End Walk" I told of a walk which, within the framework of Britain end-to-end, also footlinked the country summits of Scotland, England, Wales and Ireland. Like all big trips, it had some effect on what followed. Writing the book was harder than the walking, but it did remind me of one drawback to being footloose and fancy free—you are restricted to a very narrow line of exploration. A bike would allow far more to be seen and, after all, we Broon boys had grown up cycling every holiday as our way to explore hills, from Killarney to Kinlochbervie. I decided to cyclelink

A Cycle Link of the
Country Summits

BEN NEVIS

SNAEFELL

SCAFELL
PIKE

CARRAUN-
TOOHIL

SNOWDON

the country summits. I had no touring bike, but this was no
hindrance. I flew out to Ireland, bought one there, and began on the
Macgillycuddy Reeks.

The Reeks are often reekie—in the Auld Reekie sense—for they
face the brunt of transatlantic weather. One reason for starting there
was that "west winds never fail in Ireland." So it seemed. After a gey
dreich ascent of Carrauntoohil I was birled half way across
Ireland with a big tail wind. However, big winds usually end in big
wets and the second half took three days of grim struggle fighting
into Force 11 rain—coming out of the east!

I had waterproofs of the magical Goretex Berghaus material
(which lets sweat out, but no rain in) and Bogtrotters on my feet, so
was impervious to rain and green-tinted puddles (lots of cows in
Ireland). It was good not to end the days soaked. I was twice blown
over by the wind.

The weather cleared up for Wales, and Snowdon went in a
memorable traverse of the whole horseshoe ridge. All the country
summits are fine mountains, but suffer from the popular lure of the
highest. Ben Nevis must be Britain's highest midden. Snowdon had a
cafe on top. Tut, tut, but I enjoyed my beer!

The route went on to Chester, the walled, medieval city which has
been a favourite since I spent some National Service time on an RAF
station nearby, and then wended out to Birkenhead and the ferry to
Liverpool, to avoid the flat and industrialised Lancashire region
northwards. The diversion took me to the Isle of Man for a week.
Perhaps Snaefell there could be claimed as an additional country
summit. A cycle was a good way of exploring the Isle of Man,
though we also used tram, steam train, boat and mountain railway,
as well as biking and hiking. This is a land with the same Celtic-
Norse history as our own west. It once belonged to Scotland. Scots
feel very much at home in Man.

Anything less Scottish than Lakeland would be hard to imagine.
From Heysham-Morecambe I dawdled on by the peculiar Silverdale
limestone country and visited the railway museum at Carnforth to
see the Flying Sctsman (but it was off on a flying visit to Scotland),
then, at Windermere, we met the blare and glare of people
pressure—non-stop din, dangerous roads, the very bustle, which
ostensibly the millions had gone to the Lakes to escape. The Scafells

Carrauntoohil (left) and Beenkeragh, Ireland's highest peaks. A view along the Macgillycuddy Reeks

gave one of the hottest traverses I have ever known. It was a sweaty run to Keswick. So the peace of that evening there is a fond memory.

Cycling is all ups and downs—geographic, mechanical, mental and meteorological and at Carlisle the next day some bike repairs were needed, but the unexpectedly small bill set me flying into Galloway, the 76 miles the longest day of the trip. Kendoon was such a quiet wee hostel after the child-warfare establishments of Lakeland.

In Ayr, I had a spectacular "down" and a spectacular "up." At the busiest crossroads I had to swerve to avoid being hit by a car breenging across lanes. This turned my front wheel right round and catapulted me over the handlebars. I picked myself up unscathed, but carried off what looked like a pile of scrap, or a modern sculpture. The "up" was watching the sun set behind the serrated shape of Arran, one of the most spectacular sunsets I have ever seen, anywhere.

Two days later I crossed to Arran (with a new front wheel), then crossed over to Kintyre and up that rich cradle-land of Scottish history to Oban, crossed to Lismore, explored it and crossed back to Appin and up to Lochaber and a good day on Ben Nevis. This was by far the most enjoyable part of the trip. "East, west, hame's best." is often true.

19. *The happiness of the long-distance skier*

ACTIVE minority ski-ing is more than just going up and down the slopes of an urbanised resort. It is a branch of mountaineering.

By mountaineering I mean the fullest enjoyment of high places in all seasons. A climber may not be a mountaineer—plenty of Sheffield lads, for example, are expert climbers on the local crag gymnasiums but never go near hills as such. A skier may not be a mountaineer—plenty of pretty people commute up and down Coire Cas who would not know one end of a compass from the other. On the other hand, a mountaineer can enjoy every aspect of the hills, incuding downhill, resort ski-ing.

You will see plenty of them on the slopes of Meall a' Bhuiridh, Glen Coe's ski centre, a much more demanding and interesting skiers' mountain than Cairn Gorm. It is probably popular because of the toughness. But the mountaineers' minority-interest ski-ing takes the enthusiast well away from the clang of mechanical uplift and shrieks of the colourful tyros on the piste.

Ski-touring has been having a boom in the last few years and this winter it has not been uncommon to see tracks doing the rounds of the local golf course. I snatched a delightful hour in some woods above Dundee recently when over for an evening engagement. It was a day of crisp frost on the slopes of the Sidlaws and the snow sparked in the sun as I zipped in and out through the tree-flickering brilliance: a magic hour from busy office life made possible by the big snowfalls that most people girn about.

This touring game I first encountered in Norway where I had gone on what I thought was a rigorous training course (I was soon to try for an instructor's certificate and it seemed a good idea to panic-train in interesting new surroundings). However, it turned out to be just another holiday trip with pleasant but undemanding instruction and limited downhill facilities. Two days and you knew every piste. I bought a set of *langlauf* skis and took to the rolling hills above Geilo.

It was an enjoyable experience and, technically, far less demanding than piste/resort ski-ing. These "skinny skis" as they call them in America (here they are "touring skis") are light in weight and boots are no heavier than trainers. The fun is covering distance rather than repeating verticalities. It is very much a Scandinavian game. Everyone tours there and it was not uncommon to be passed in the middle of nowhere by whole families on skis—right down to baby being towed behind in a sledge capsule.

More than once I met such families digging into the snow seemingly at random only to hear they had their "summer houses" there and were trying to find the trap-door in the roof. They spent their weekends ski-touring from "home".

Ski-touring carries you loping over the landscape as fast as a man can run and even with a pack on your back you will travel further and faster than is possible on foot. It is the way to go winter backpacking in fact. One of the photographs shows how fruid the action is. It was taken on the approach to Carn a' Chlamain above Glen Tilt. We had climbed out of the glen, traversed this peak (once visited by Queen Victoria), and descended to stay the night at the Tarf bothy—the only one I know that hangs a AA hotel sign on its wall. Five stars that night.

The next day we did a circuit of An Sgarsach and Carn Ealar, lunched at the bothy and went out to Blair Atholl over Beinn Dearg, a day which, *a pied*, would have been very long indeed in summer and quite impossible in the deep snow of winter.

On another occasion three of us traversed over Cairn Gorm to the Fords of Avon, then skied through the Lairig an Laoigh to Beinn Bhreac above Derry, returning over Beinn a' Chaoruinn to spend the night in the Fords of Avon howff. Next day we climbed up Beinn Mheadhoin and did a circuit round to Macdhui and home to Cairn Gorm—another fabulous round which would have been impossible on foot.

The two trips were made on quite different skis. As the term "ski-touring" has been used indiscriminately for both types of activity a bit of clarification is needed. While Scandinavian touring has a long localised history (there are prehistoric cave-paintings showing skiers) the Alps saw the development of ordinary ski-ing less than a century ago, both for recreation, and eventually into an Olympic sport.

Mountaineers, who are much more solitary in outlook and who compete against nature rather than against other people, discovered

Mike "loping" on his *langlauf* skis—on Carn a' Chlamain above Glen Tilt

their own branch of Alpine ski-ing. They called it touring as well (which has led to the confusion) but as the objective was frequently to climb mountains "ski mountaining" is a clearer definition. Ski-ing *up* mountains sounds a bit improbable to most people.

I remember the first time I saw it in Scotland. Being all mountaineer my first day on skis took me up Largo Law (on 1,000 ft), my second was on a 2,000 footer, White Wisp in the Ochils, and my third bagged Stuc a' Chroin (over 3,000 ft). Climbing up was only possible carrying my skis and floundering or thrashing about on the skis at vast expenditure of energy. Yet I knew people did this regularly. There was either a knack or a method I had not discovered.

Standing above the top lift on Cairn Gorm one day I saw a man on skis calmly turn round and swish-swish straight up the hill. He did not run backwards even at what looked a ridiculous angle. I slipped out of my skis and raced after him to find the secret.

He had "skins" on the soles of his standard type skis, and bindings which could adjust to allow his heel to lift. He just "walked" uphill in the magical way I had seen.

The (artificial) skins were put on with the hairy "lay" facing back so when the skis were slid forward there was no restriction, but any tendency to run back down at the end of a stride was stopped by the skin rucking up (like stroking a cat the wrong way). There is naturally a limit to the angle of climbing and sometimes a slope may be too icy. There are actually ski crampons (*harsheisen*) which can then be attached to the skis or boots.

This is really my first love as far as ski-ing goes and days such as the Cairn Gorm one outlined above or a traverse of part of Glen Shiels's Cluanie Ridge or the peaks of the Lawers range have given mountaineering days of unequalled enjoyment.

Scotland, alas, is not all that suitable for the Scandinavian type of touring. The summit plateaux are frequently too icy, the slopes of our hills are often too steep and the valley bottoms seldom have the snow. Thanks to high-powered commercial pushing this has been put over as the great new winter sport—which it simply is not. It is an occasional bonus and good fun but I have seen a whole winter pass with my *langlauf* skis never taken out of the car.

On our climb up Beinn Mheadhoin in the Cairngorms the slope

was so icy that the hardness of the surface actually buckled the metal blades of our ski crampons. Skinny skis used in Scotland usually have metal edges on them, as do ordinary skis, to cope with icier slopes. In Scandinavia the edges are wood.

For going uphill the skinny skis use a range of waxes to gain a similar effect to skins. Changing waxes, or taking skins off and on, is a bit of a bane (cold fingers struggling in spindrift) but has been simplified over the years with skinny skis having "fishscale" soles instead and skins are now stuck rather than buckled on. In good conditions both are equally suitable on the hills.

Our trip from the Tilt involved two of us, one on skinny skis and the other on mountain skis. We ended the day more or less together and argued the pros and cons all evening. I reckon it was a draw but given nasty conditions (the normal in Scotland) the mountain skis have the edge—in more ways than the literal. Both types of touring can be enjoyed wherever there is snow. There are days when the Pentlands can provide the best in the world.

20. Canoes through the Great Glen

BEING in the hills is more important than our doings on them is one of the more heretical notions I have always had and being in the hills means moving in them, not being static. Thus I have had a certain impatience with rock-climbing or winter-climbing while other aspects like ski-ing, sailing, pony-trekking, canoeing, have enthused only as means to an end, not an end in themselves.

Ski-ing to me is not the urban squalor of the Cairnwell or Cairn Gorm, it is using skis to cross country, either at home or in outlandish places like the High Atlas Mountains of Morocco. It is journeying. Apart from viewing ponies as being dangerous at both ends and uncomfortable in the middle I feel the normal ponytrekking is pathetic day-plodding. A coast-to-coast with ponies—that would be the real thing! Sailing lends itself more naturally to travelling on and the months I've had on the *Captain Scott* and *The Eye of the Wind* have provided some of the best memories of a lifetime of stravaiging.

My pedestrian ploddings have carried me all over the mountainy regions, the most basic progression of all, and the easiest to lose in a world that runs on wheels. Canoeing, too is a grand adjunct to mountain travel and Scotland has lochs, rivers and coastline for a lifetime of canoe expeditions. I try and do something with the canoe each year, apart from the ninety-ninth trip to Inchkeith which is the home circuit.

My canoe normally causes raised eyebrows among the plastic water generation of today. It is a sturdy, heavy, thirty-year-old kit-built canvas-on-wooden frame job. It cost me £5 and has been down most Scottish rivers, on many lochs and made long sea expeditions. I know if it goes over that I can right it and climb back in, even in a gale, even with what feels like a ton of camping and hill gear on board. I love the old witch dearly.

Like any female, she takes some looking after, some pampering. Many tins of paint have added to her weight, beauty and watertight state. But she always wants something else. This year I added a hinged back-rest and several hooks for shock cords across the deck to carry spare paddles and other gear, including a collapsible trolley

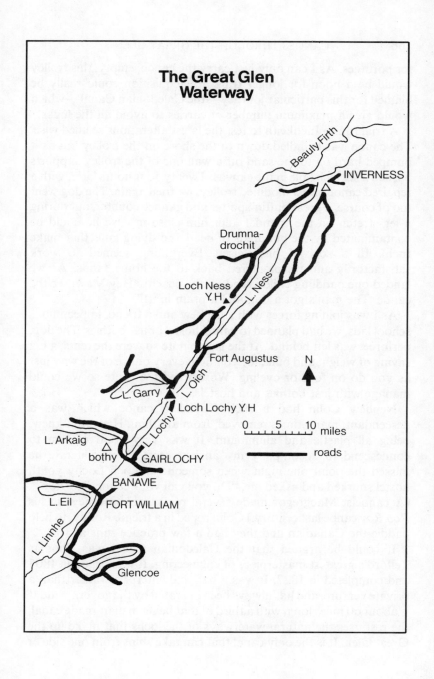

The Great Glen
Waterway

Beauly Firth

INVERNESS

Drumna-
drochit

Loch Ness
Y. H

L. Ness

Fort Augustus

N

L. Oich

L. Garry

Loch Lochy Y. H

L. Lochy

0   5   10 miles

L. Arkaig

bothy

GAIRLOCHY

roads

BANAVIE

L. Eil

FORT WILLIAM

L. Linnhe

Glencoe

for portages. As I can only just carry the canoe, empty, this trolley would be a boon for longer trips. Its acquisition could really be blamed for this particular journey—the Caledonian Canal—which would give a maximum number of carries to avoid all the locks.

A trial run to Inchkeith to test the latest alterations seemed wise. The canoe was trundled down to the shore on the trolley but as it bumped hard on to the sand off a wall one of the trolley supports bashed a six inch hole in the canvas. Twenty-four hours later, with a repaired canoe and a modified trolley, we tried again. The dog went too of course, a great puffin-spotter and gannet-counter, but during a leg-stretch on the island I kept him close in case he could be contaminated by the hundreds of dead and dying gulls that make Inchkeith a sort of bird-Belsen. Everything seemed to work satisfactorily and we ploutered back to the home sands. As we landed one paddling child yelled up the beach: "Hey Maw, see the canoe. The man's got a dug and a pram in it!"

As I was joining forces with a nephew and a friend, impecunious school lads, we had planned to camp, hostel or use bothies. The dog, perforce, was left behind. At the last minute so were the tents, a big saving of weight and bulk, for you fight every ounce of the way just as you do on foot or cycling. We worked the route so we could manage with just bothies and hostels.

Nephew Colin had a slick Canadian canoe which was a descendant, many times removed, from anything Hiawatha knew, being all plastic and aluminium. It was very good of him to condescend to accompany my ancient craft. Being illiterate he missed the point one night when someone at Loch Lochy youth hostel smirked and asked me, "Do you call your canoe *Rob Roy*?" (A canoeist Macgregor made several remarkable journeys in his *Rob Roy* canoe last century.) Colin roped in a friend, Roddy, to help paddle the Canadian and they had a few practice runs as well.

It could be argued that the Caledonian Canal was Thomas Telford's greatest masterpiece of engineering. It was begun in 1803 and completed in 1822. It was a national enterprise rather than a private venture, and has always been operated by the government. It is about 60 miles long, with a third of that being in man-made canal, the rest uses the natural waterways of the lochs that make up the Great Glen. It is the only canal that can take ships from one side of the country to the other. "There are 15 locks to the summit from Corpach, and 16 from Inverness, each raising any ship for 8 ft." I quote, for my modest arithmetic is rather puzzled by those statistics. Is the sea really 8 ft higher at Loch Linnhe than at the Beauly Firth?

The definitive book on the canal, still in print, is A.D. Cameron's "The Caledonian Canal", published by Terence Dalton Ltd. It is a social, historical and engineering saga of great interest. Telford was attempting a work years ahead of its time. He often had to invent the machinery to do the job, and to operate the canal. It was a great undertaking but—sounds familiar—it took longer and cost more than originaly estimated. It was completed just in time to be obsolete.

The Great Glen has several youth hostels: Glen Nevis, Loch Lochy, Alltsaigh (Loch Ness) and Inverness but the first and last of these are usually mobbed in summer by the international hitchers so we largely used the other two. The first day saw our canoes taken north and a cache of food laid by a loch west of the Great Glen. We spent the night at Loch Lochy youth hostel (which runs canoeing courses) and early the next day went to Corpach harbour office for our permits before launching. Rather than start at the sea lock and shortly after have the huge flight of seven locks, "Neptune's staircase" to carry round, we started above them, at Banavie.

It was a place of memories, especially as we saw the Sea Cadet training ship *Royalist* going down the locks. She and the *Eye of the Wind* had been alongside there a few years previously: two tall ships in the canal was surely an unusual sight. On that occasion I had taken some of the crew of *Eye of the Wind* for an overnight climb of Ben Nevis.

The brooding hill was crisp and clear this morning too. We took to the oily dark waters beside a big Danish ship *Opal* which greeted us by starting her engines which then blew out a series of smoke rings with every putt-putt of the motors.

After an hour's paddling along the smooth canal we landed for a few minutes to rest arms and bottoms (the parts which feel the work of canoeing) but the midges soon had us back on the water. *Opal* passed. A fishing boat passed. At Gairlochy (locks and swing bridge) we used the wheels, in turn, and were sitting having a picnic when they passed again—with some interesting double takes. Our rate of progress was about 4½ mph so even the holiday cruisers, at 6 mph, quickly overhauled us. As we paddled out into Loch Lochy we ran into a stiff breeze. This reach was originally the river but a new cutting was made for the river and this goes down to Mucomer power station, then under a fine Telford bridge to join the Spean.

It was rougher than the lads had met previously but in the middle of a big loch there are fairly limited options. The prospect of drowning, as much as hanging, "concentrates the mind marvellously." We battled on for two hours to eventually land on the west shore. It was hot enough for Roddy to spend much of the time in the loch while Colin and I trundled my canoe off on a two-mile portage. "At least there were no midges underwater."

Colin walked back with the wheels and they brought his canoe along. I had meanwhile retrieved the cache from the forest. It had been tied in a waterproof bag and hung from a tree, not, as one of them suggested, to keep it from bears but to keep it from equally destructive mice. A dixie of tea was waiting the boys' arrival. In the time we had taken for this double portage the wind had risen considerably.

The gale hit us on the starboard bow and reduced a two-mile paddle to an exhausting hour-long battle. It was a relief to reach land. We ran on to the bank of water lobelia and leapt out into knee-deep mud. Never was a bothy more welcome. We carried our gear over to it and set about the serious business of eating the evening away—easy enough for teenagers after a long first day's canoeing. The free-ranging garrons tried their best to join us inside. They didn't seem to like midges either.

The midges had been behind our decision to find buildings for the night, rather than camp and the next day the boys forcefully got the message. The bothy was reduced to something like Rorke's Drift with the midge impis attacking ferociously. We spent the day climbing Beinn Bhan. The summit gave a long view of our route and nodded across to Ben Nevis.

The midges also plagued our departure from the bothy next morning but, by the time we had reversed the portages, Loch Lochy was windy and wet and became ever more so as we progressed. The wind was more or less behind us and we surged and surfed along in

The Eye of the Wind anchored in Loch Ness at the Fort Augustus locks up to the Caledonian Canal

fine style. After an hour we were so chilled we landed to don waterproofs and brewed some tea. Any idea of climbing the Munros above the loch were torn to shreds just as the clouds were being ripped up by the gale.

We reached Laggan Locks far too early: a good excuse to guzzle and fester in the renowned tearoom. Its walls had pictures of the canal in early days and quite by chance, on a previous visit in 1976 I saw the locks empty for repairs—only the second time ever. The huge arched hole emphasised the scale of the canal. It was built for ships. We canoeists did not count at all and had to carry round. The difficult cutting from here to Loch Oich is the highest reach on the Caledonian Canal at 106 ft. A mile on up the tree-hidden canal we landed, just one field away from the comforts of friendly Loch Lochy youth hostel.

My first Braehead canoeing trip in the Great Glen had been based there twenty years before and the same kindly warden, Mrs Fraser, was there to greet the next generation. Jane Wilson was running the canoe courses for the SYHA and summed up their hefty day to Fort Augustus-and-back as "Rain. Rain all day and then a gale coming back. It was great!" A twelve-year-old from Musselburgh, Jonathan Mackay, had been one of the party and buzzed with energy after such a day. I noted our pair retired early to bed. There were plenty of drookit cyclists as well as canoeists but Mrs Fraser and her cheery assistant made everyone at home. The fire alarm went off three times in the night (accidentally), but Colin and Roddy did not even hear it.

The weather cheered up for Loch Oich. We stopped at the Well of the Heads, that uniquely blood-thirsty memorial that comes up to port not long after the swing bridge. While many know something of the tale of murder and revenge and the seven renegade heads being washed in the well before delivery to the chief at Glengarry Castle, few realise the well still exists. It is under the road but there is a passage in to it from the shore of Loch Oich—which few notice. We landed beside it, but ice-cream in the shop rather than historic interest motivated the landfall.

Dredging Loch Oich set Telford some problems and Alastair MacDonnell of Glengarry was a thorn in the flesh. This is the chief still famous because of the resplendent portrait by Raeburn in the National Gallery. He did not like a canal passing his castle.

Coming ashore on Loch Lochy during the trip through the Great Glen

There was hardly any water flowing over the weir into the River Oich so there was no temptation to run it. We once did with some school lads from Fife and as we swept past the lawns of a mansion house a high-faluting voice trilled "What do you think you're doing?" to which the blockhead at the rear returned the perfect rejoiner "Canoeing!"—and vanished round the bend.

Two locks, Cullochy and Kyltra, break the placid canal before Fort Augustus. At Kyltra the keeper once allowed us to pick rhubarb from his garden for the time it took *Eye of the Wind* to pass through the lock. Rhubarb rained down on the decks. Fort Augustus greeted us with a pipe band. It was actually gala day and the Lochaber Pipe Band, a traction engine and various other oddities ensured a crowd of people, through which we wheeled our canoes to the pepper-pot lighthouse at the south end of Loch Ness. The pipe band still marched and played and when the tannoy music from the abbey grounds began poor Colin winced at the competitive cacophony (he is pipe major of his school band.)

We felt remote lookers-on at all these festivities, being set apart for tougher challenges as it were—which took all our concentration and effort. Being water-borne set us aside from the bustle of life on road and in village. The five locks of Fort Augustus run down through the village so the two sides meet rather brutally.

It was sunny again and two more Danish schooners arrived:*Jens Krogh* from Loch Ness, and *Grena*—when the festivities eventually allowed the swing bridge to open. *Grena* tied up opposite us and one figure stripped off and had a splash-bath on deck. A rich Glasgow voice from the picnic next to ours screeched, "Wid ye credit thaat? She's nae got ony claes on at aa!" to which came the reply "Dinna be daft, hen. I've never seen you tak a shoor wi yir claes oan!" The boys probably thought I was choking on my sardine sandwich.

We went on to use the strong tail wind. Any help up Loch Ness is welcome. It is a loch of some monotony we decided. The scenery changes very little over many miles. Any point was welcome to give a lee respite from the surge. We twice landed just to ease numb bums and weary shoulders, before reaching Alltsaigh youth hostel, an old favourite which looks over the loch so it is like being on board ship.

Mrs Maclean signed us in for two nights, for on the following day we had only eight miles instead of today's score. We would leave the canoes at Drumnadrochit Bay and bus back to the hostel, then reverse the procedure the next day. The canoes were actually left near Castle Urquhart, out of sight and our paddles and jackets were hidden in the bracken. It was odd to go and catch a bus.

The castle has had one of the stormiest of histories and little enough remains but the towers and battlements set on the knoll over Loch Ness makes it a magnet for the tourists. We paddled around to take photographs from the loch. The only other landmark on the short day had been the cairn in memory of John Cobb, holder of the land speed record, who died trying to achieve a new water record on Loch Ness. This is the largest volume of water in Britain and it is a loch that is seldom placid.

Off Urquhart Castle Loch Ness reaches its deepest point, almost 1,000 ft, which is deeper than the North Sea. Drumnadrochit has an exhibition which goes into the mystery of the "monster". A great deal of serious research goes on but whatever the scientists argue one way or another it does the tourist trade no harm. I wish there was a better word than "monster" though.

The rest of Loch Ness gave us our only head wind so it was hard work with little to catch the imagination. "Non-scenery" someone called it. We were glad to rest at Lochend, below the house that has an inland lighthouse attached upstairs. The tour boats seemed to be busy: *Jacobite Lady* and *Jacobite Chieftain* and *Scott II* passing us there. The last set up a big wash just as the Canadian was being launched. Two big waves caught Colin right below the chin and ran down inside his life jacket. It was the only wetting of the trip while involved with the canoes. Roddy and I enjoyed it.

Loch Dochfour is small and pretty and we could actually hear the weir where the River Ness left it. Dochgarroch was our last lock, the only change in level from away back at Fort Augustus, and the last finishing flight at Muirtown seven miles on, which we would avoid by completing the trip above them. Dochgarroch was lifeless apart from two children fishing with the traditional bent pins. A notice pinned on the keeper's "box" said "gone to lunch, back at 1.30". We were obviously nearing civilisation. You could tell by the cans floating in the canal.

This was another length that proved difficult to construct and for some 500 yards the bottom was lined with locally-woven cloth which was then plastered in a clay-based "puddle" to make a waterproof barrier that is still effective over 150 years later. Telford is such a ubiquitous figure in Scotland with his record of roads, bridges, 30 churches and manses, harbours and canals that we tend to forget just how long ago he lived. It was the period of the Napoleonic Wars that saw the Caledonian Canal built.

Tomnahurich Hill appeared: "one of the most picturesque burial grounds in the country" as the guide book declared. Below it was the swing bridge where we hauled out the canoes for the last time, below it was the municipal camp site where we rushed my canoe along and booked the eighth-last plot available. I then rushed off (still in squelching canoe shoes) and just caught the Fort William bus— back to Loch Lochy youth hostel where my camping-car had been left. Once back, we pitched a tent for the boys, and the thunderstorm broke that somehow seemed to end our 67-mile journey and also the 67 days of that hot summer.

21. Inchkeith, Island of dereliction

BEFORE going off to canoe the Caledonian Canal I had a quick paddle out to Inchkeith to see everything was in working order. It was, fortunately, and Inchkeith proved its usual variety of interests. It was not a solitary trip.

You could almost judge the distance by the bird life. There was a diving world of gannets first, then the flurry-scurry of solemn puffins, then the cliff-cacophony of gulls. Porpoises surfacing just behind the canoe nearly gave the dog and I heart failure. The cormorants were hung out to dry on the skerries as we turned in to the harbour.

Alongside were the Sea Cadets' boat, a fishing boat and several yachts. A skin-diver was splashing along, and four boys were birling about in a dinghy. It was like something out of Arthur Ransome and one could almost believe in Inchkeith as a children's adventure playground.

But that was an oily-calm day on a Sunday morning in the holidays. A cliff-girt island at the mercy of the weather, covered in derelict fortifications and diseased birdlife is hardly a promising place for that sort of proposed development, especially in today's economic climate. Those of us who live in or by the Firth of Forth had a quiet chuckle when the sales blurb suggested it would make a pleasant place to stay and commute to Edinburgh. It is the seabirds who do that, with fatal results. Rummaging in Edinburgh's rubbish results on botulism and in dry summers like the last one the result is gull corpses all over the island. I counted over fifty dead birds while walking up to the lighthouse.

When Carlyle visited Inchkeith he mentioned the keepers having families with them and pasturing cows. It was *L'ile des Chevaux* to the French troops garrisoned there in the sixteenth century because their horses thrived on the grass. I don't think horses or cows would appreciate it now and the keepers' families have lived in Edinburgh for many years. The light is going to be made automatic so even the cheery keepers will depart. It will then be left to the white-washing seabirds. Perhaps it should be made into an effective, controlled bird island. Whatever happens the gulls desperately need to be culled.

Lighthouses are oddly pleasant objects, which is just as well

175

considering their conspicuous nature. Inchkeith flickers its light across my bedroom window of nights—or blasts us with its scrawny new foghorn. When the foghorn started in 1899 it blared continuously for 139 hours before being turned off the Fife shore to face the sea.

Our resident starlings are excellent mimics (they can even make the sound of the garage door skarting across the concrete drive) so when I noticed one doing a very good peewit imitation I grabbed a tape-recorder and switched on. After a few mintues the bird flew off and I rewound to play what I'd picked up. It came loud and clear all right—the blare of Inchkeith! It takes several diesels to build up the pressure for the blast so it is best heard from some miles away.

The first mention of a light is 1635 when, at a May Island submission for a light, Inchkeith was also mentioned. The May got their's the next year. Inchkeith had to wait 170 years. When they did begin, no time was lost, for construction started in May 1803 and the light was lit in September 1804. Perhaps because of its closeness to Edinburgh, quite a few innovations were introduced at Inchkeith over the years. The optics and mechanics are a bit beyond me, but R.W. Munro's "Scottish Lighthouses" is the easiest source book in general. Inchkeith, both generally and for its light, is covered in a booklet by David Marshall, *L'île des Chevaux,* which was issued in 1983. (One of the Inchkeith lights was later installed at Cape Spear in Newfoundland, the most westerly point in America.)

The name Inchkeith probably derives from connections with the Earl Marischal family. A Caithness chief was granted the island in 1010 for his help in defeating the Danes. It was forfeited from them in the reign of James V and given to Sir Andrew Wood of Largo, who was governor during the "Rough Wooing" by Henry VIII of England. It remained a defensive base from that time to fairly recently.

Mary Queen of Scots was hustled off to France rather than marrying Henry's son Edward (one of the interesting IFs of history, had it come off) but Edward's "Protector" Somerset seized Inchkeith during his Pinkie campaign and French troops had a bloody time regaining control. A dated stone of 1564 marked its rebuilding, and although little remains this stone now is inserted over a gateway in the lighthouse's courtyard.

Sunday morning on the Forth—in the harbour on Inchkeith Island

It changed hands many times and really only became a military base again in 1860 when batteries were built and these were increased early this century so that Leith, Inchkeith and Kinghorn formed an unattractive array of guns for any sea marauders.

As my home stands on the site of one of the shore batteries I feel a certain involvement with this history. (A neighbour has turned a bunker into an underground billiard room!) Inchkeith was more used during the Second World War, since when time, decay and vandalism have left the island neglected, overgrown and derelict.

On a previous paddle out to Inchkeith I jokingly said I'd bring back a ladder or something to complete a stile over the garden fence. We came back towing a fishing boat's companionway and several other beachcombed items. Inchkeith is still a fearsome place for shipping. The skerries facing Lothian are particulary bad, being completely covered at high tide. Now they are marked by the hulk of the *Switha* which ran aground there a few years ago. Inchkeith is a sad place now: "a suitable case for treatment." as they say.

As I can be seasick in my canoe the lure of tall ships extracts a penalty for any indulgence in such adventuring. "Nelson was seasick everytime he put to sea" is no comfort really but one goes just the same. Tall ships offer one of the few real adventures lingering on from past centuries. For all too brief years the tops'l schooner Captain Scott *sailed our Scottish waters and for several months of November in a row I joined the crew for what were sea-bound Outward Bound courses.*

Alas, nobody would pay the price of a quarter of a mile of motorway to keep her operating in Britain; the Scott *was sold off to the Arabs and now sails warmer waters, renamed* Youth of Oman. *What a commentary on this country! I thought my days of deep-water sailing were over but luck decreed otherwise. I have heaved up over several lee rails since those stormy days in the Minch or Pentland Firth.*

22. Tall ship and high mountains

"OPERATION DRAKE" was planned as a round-the-world passage to commemorate the four hundredth anniversary of Drake's voyage. The *Captain Scott* was first choice of ship before she was sold to the Arabs and the brigantine *The Eye of the Wind* became base and flagship, setting off on the circumnavigation in the autumn of 1978. Her crew were sponsored youngsters between the age of eighteen and twenty two.

The ship was built in 1911 and seemed doomed after a fire in Sweden but some enthusiasts restored her—with superb wood from a dance floor, a bank and a church and later a deck rescued from a destroyer in the breakers' yard. The ship was a beauty and I'd followed Operation Drake's progress with interest. (Operation Raleigh is on similar lines).

Various projects were undertaken on the way and at remote regions ashore. These ranged from simple visits to complex scientific work involving many other people. If the sailing had affinities with Drake, there were also startling differences. Old and new constantly met on the voyage. None of the "Young Explorers" could but gain

179

from their experiences.

Becoming a young explorer was not easy. Too many wanted to join. Competitive selection produced the nine four-month teams for these phases, about 250 lucky young men and women out of 50,000 applicants.

By odd coincidence I became involved in the last shore expedition to Morocco. Earlier in the year two of the Operation Drake staff from London had taken part in the Ultimate Challenge coast-to-coast walk and we met when we had finished at the Park Hotel in Montrose. There they discovered that I spent several months each year in Morocco, so as the voyage's last port of call, for re-rigging the ship was Gibraltar, Morocco was chosen for an expedition—and I was asked to lead the Young Explorers.

The visit to Morocco would be brief, but it was hoped in the time available to visit the magical city of Marrakech, explore the Berber way of life in the High Atlas and perhaps climb Jbel Toubkal, 4167 metres, the highest peak in North Africa.

After crossing by hydrofoil from Gibraltar, one Kenyan lad was refused entry as he had no visa—and had to sail on to Spain. An evening and a morning were spent in Tangier before the long train journey south. At six the next morning the palms and thousand-year old mud ramparts of Marrakech were outlined against the horizon of peaks. We had made it. The "Marrakech Express" was for real!

The party carried their gear across the waking city to the Hotel de Foucauld where a welcome breakfast was soon produced. It is difficult to convey the feeling of this old city. The hotel is on the edge of the Medina and in its teeming alleys and squares life must have changed little since the days of Drake.

Trade guilds of metal-workers, leather-workers, wood carvers, kaftan makers, jewellers, carpet traders all occupy areas and frantic buying and selling, bargaining and arguing goes on all day. On the main square as the day cools, the crowds gather round the story-tellers, quack doctors, snake charmers, Mauretanian dancers, sweetmeat sellers—a bedlam of sound and a dazzle of colour.

The Young Explorers found it fascinating. They stayed on a rooftop vantage point till dusk, with the sun setting behind the minaret of the Koutoubia and the tomb of the city founders. This

The young girls of Imlil dancing at the Fete du Trone at Asni

city was here before William became the Conqueror. A Moroccan meal ended an exciting day.

In the morning a hired bus took the party into the mountains: thirty miles across the plains, up through forested foothills and finally a dirt road to the village of Imlil where an alpine hut was used as a base.

A great welcome was given to everyone—usually ending up in some local house for mint tea. The party operated in three groups for cooking and other organising needs. The first snows of winter had brushed the peaks and the walnut leaves were sun-yellow with fresh autumn painting. An enchanting setting for the perched villages rimming the road-end at Imlil.

There was hardly a moment when there was not the sound of singing from the girls and shouts from the men as they ploughed with mules for the autumn sowing. A whole way of life was refreshingly revealed to the youngsters from Britain, Canada, Australia and other places. Sharon Crockett from Largs was the only other Scot in the party. Imlil is 1750 metres. Deliciously cool after the plains.

At dawn the next morning a procession wound up the valley, past the kasbah, past the plain of Around where they had seen dancing at a wedding the night before, and on to the shrine where the locals produced more welcome mint tea. The worship at saints' shrines and even animistic beliefs still linger in the mountains despite being officially Islamic. Central government is a long way off, however, and the mountain Berber is independent and self-reliant. (Kirkwall and London are much the same!).

As height was gained the weather began to break down. By the time we reached the Neltner Hut, at 3150 metres it was snowing, bitter cold for folk who had just come through the Red Sea. Without mountain gear the chances of anything further seemed hopeless.

Luckily it cleared in the night, and at dawn, all those who could, set off. One or two with just plimsoles stayed in the hut. The new snow, drifted over the boulder fields and ravines, made for slow progress. Some people simply had stockings instead of mits and plastic bags tied round ankles to try to keep out the snow.

Everyone who set out finally made the Tizi-n-Ouagane on the main spine of the mountains, at 3725 metres, higher than many famous peaks in the Alps. Beyond lay a sea of cloud. The Sahara!

A small party went up to another col and spent the rest of the day on a classic rock climbing route but lack of equipment and time eventually forced them down. They walked into the hut just as supper was being served! Five were keen enough, experienced enough and fit enough to try for Toubkal itself the next day, while everyone else returned to Imlil.

After dark one party went to a local village for *cous cous,* the national dish (a stew on a cornflour base). They returned to find the five had climbed Toubkal—the highest summit north of Kenya. All the objectives had been gained.

The bus back out stopped at Asni and everyone had coffee in the deluxe Hotel de Toubkal, resplendent in fresh craftmanship and with a garden bright with roses—and a view to the Atlas Mountains. The end, it felt, for the bus dropped the party at Marrakech Station.

All that was left was to swop off all surplus food, clothing, boots—anything—to gain carpets and kaftans, pottery and drums, leather bags and djellabas.

Marrakech and the mountains faded into dusk as the party set off on the 15-hour overnight train journey to Tangier. They arrived in rain and the hydrofoil took three hours instead of one to deliver the young explorers to Gibraltar and the ship. That really brought the expedition down to earth.

There was hardly time to tell tall stories, before the tall ship sailed off. The rigger Wullie Buchanan, who had prepared her for the windy miles of the North Atlantic (and the return to a Royal welcome in London) and I stood a deal forlornly on the quay as *The Eye of the Wind* hoisted sail after sail and headed out into the fanfare of sunset.

Having been directly involved with The Eye of the Wind, *yet not sailing in her, made that a sad parting at Gibraltar. However Lady Luck stepped in again. The ship was refurbished after* Operation Drake *and before setting off to her Australian/Pacific cruising waters she had a shake-down run to Scotland. I was asked to join her at Oban for a trip through the Great Glen to Loch Ness and back. Loathe to leave I stayed aboard to Bristol. The* Operation Drake *trainees had so enthused about Morocco that it was decided to sail via Casablanca rather than the Azores. If I were to sail out with them would I in turn show the crew Marrakech and the mountains? So it happened. You have probably gathered from the peppering of Moroccan references that I am an enthusiast for that bustling country—so one trip in the High Atlas has to be included. The* Scotsman *often goes abroad.*

23. The Agoundis Valley

"SOMETHING lost behind the Ranges . . . lost and waiting for you. Go!" It was Kipling who wrote that line which has always spiced my gingerbread of life. The poem ends: "Anybody might have found it, but—His whisper came to me."

Kipling could have been writing about the hidden Agoundis Valley. I sincerely hope you have *not* heard of it, or Kipling fails me, and I fail you. It is a real IF-country.

One of the joys of Morocco, perhaps its most persuasive charm, is the vivid quality of contrast. The High Atlas Mountains slap up from the desert to snowy mountains, not far from the bustling, magical city of Marrakesh, whose city walls were built before our Alexander III had a riding accident. I think it is the most fascinating city anywhere but the Kipling call is too strong when you can look off to that horizon. I head for it year after year.

A small group of us had been skiing, climbing and trekking, first in the Middle Atlas cedar forests (the only place where I've *skied* into a

184

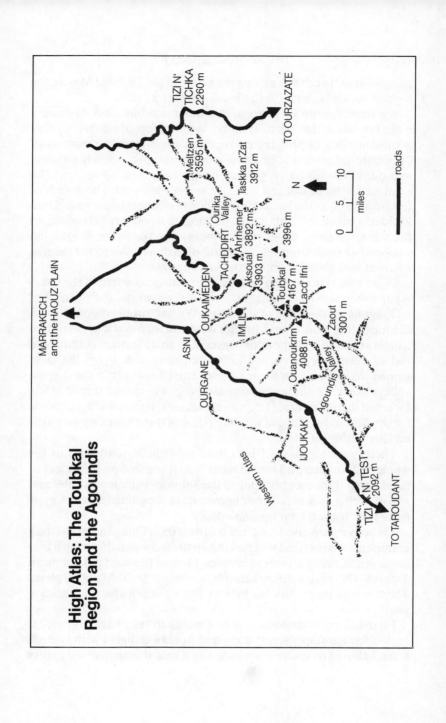

High Atlas: The Toubkal Region and the Agoundis

party of apes!) and then among the giants of the Toubkal Massif, the highest summits, lying to the south of Marrakech.

We were shut up by a storm in a mountain hut for a day and a night but out of that peculiar limbo-world of forced inactivity came a stunning day of primary colours and sheer primitive exaltation. (The spiritual often reaches the summits through the purely physical and our climb left us very much on the heights in all senses.) We climbed Jbel Toubkal, and it felt the top of the world. Thousands of feet below us was the Lac d'Ifni, a blue eye of water in the wasteland. I told of a bivouac beside it with us lying on the sunny side while, on the other, the snow calved mini-icebergs into the water. A local lad swopped us fresh trout for a handful of matches. We rolled them in oatmeal and grilled them on the hot embers.

I was also able to point out the deep, sinuous course of the Oued Agoundis, the River Agoundis, which rises on the col of the Tizi n'Ouagane on the spine of the Atlas. We had dropped down to it a decade before from a peak further west and followed it up. We hired a mule and used it till the poor beast could go no further. A thousand feet of destructive scree led to its trembling end. From the crest gained we looked on a scene of utter emptiness only in the deepest valleys like a virus lodged in a cracked cup, was there a thread of life. I wanted then to return. Here was the chance. I preached my crusade for the Agoundis. It ended with our party of three amicably going off on three different ploys!

There were no maps. I borrowed a Michelin road map of the whole of Morocco and traced what little it showed on half a leaf of toilet paper. I thoroughly applied the Shipton-Tilman principles and set off with a rucksack for unknown days weighing less than most folks take for a tramp up Snowdon.

The other two used skis up to the Tizi n'Ouagane and I had crampons. An icy wind was picking up the snow and throwing it into the south, forming a sneer of cornice. I hoped the wind did not mean a storm. There is a certain rectitude in adding "Insh' Allah" to plans. There are as many "ifs" in hills as there are prickles on a prickly pear.

I handed my crampons over to Charles to take back and set off armed for ice slope, scree, dogs and human dangers with one ski stick. I skirted to where a pinnacle like a split thumb allowed access to the snows below. They were still frozen so I tiptoed down then, when safe, sat on top of my rucksack and tobogganed down into the corrie of the valley head.

Suddenly I was very much alone: Dave's red *duvet* was a tiny dot on the crag above, great cliffs swept in on the corniced walls of the pass and the spindrift licked about my boots. The sugary taste of fear was in my mouth so there was a wave and a shouted insult, then off for the Agoundis, whose waters were deep below the squeaking snow. I planned basically to follow its course to where it crossed the Tizi n'Test motor road, one of only two roads to break through the great chain of the High Atlas. From there I would return to Marrakech.

The Agoundis though on the south side of the spine of the Atlas, sidling along below summits 4,000 metres high, joins the Nfis River at Ijoukak on the Test road and somehow breaks through to the north. It ends as a dotted line on the map: those melting snows might not even reach the sea.

The valley fell steeply in a succession of corries, determinedly down, down, pressed between the limbs of rock, until the river broke out from under the snow. The crags of the gorge were draped with icicle teeth. They gleamed in the sun and here and there, one had been broken off. There is only one winner in the battle between ice and sun.

Odd cairns showed a summer line but vanished when needed to denote a way through a constriction of the valley, which closed in to a gap (no wider than a road), jammed with boulders and noisy waters. I picked a way down the slabby crags and crossed the stream. At the moment of impasse a ledge led out across the cliff to easy ground.

It was noon, and after a week unwashed, I was decidedly high, so off came long johns for an icy splash. Drying in the hot sun was all right!

On that previous visit we had hit the Agoundis at its last village, then come well up before leaving over a pass, the Tizi n'Zaout (where the mule had given up) so I expected to join known country soon. After another craggy traverse I was amazed to find a *seguia* (irrigation channel) leading off. It flowed strongly but bands of snow soon blocked it. The horizontal line of the duct could be seen running on a couple of miles to cross a col, so some village in the arid south would enjoy summer water. The channel had been carved or built along slopes that were almost precipice in places. From that col two miles off, easy scree slopes dropped down to the Agoundis, so I decided to follow the *seguia*, then descend to the river. The col proved to be the Tizi n'Zaout for, once there, the view was instantly recalled.

Jbel Siroua, an extinct volcano was Highland blue beyond a maze .of foothills and plateaux—the whole stippled white.

The *seguia* was enjoyed largely in retrospect. At one stage it was so cut into the rock that I had to crawl, hoping the twenty foot wall supporting it had been well constructed.

Kipling uses the term "go-fever" and I succumbed to this. Beyond the col the ridge undulated up into a fine peak, the Adrar Tirkout, which we had admired on our summit two days back. It could surely be traversed?

Beyond, forming the south side of the Agoundis, lay a long ridge, its flanks both precipitous and snowy but I hoped a side valley would give a breach in these defences. If it did not then I would really be out on a limb sawing away. It had the additional attraction of sinning. If I did not turn up Charles could do something about searching the Agoundis but now I was going to wander along unknown mountain tops, not down the valley.

There is nothing like the necessity of not breaking a leg to ensure you don't, especially if you are certain the vultures would find you before any friend, or foe. The miles of undulating ridge brought home the Atlas lesson that what looks easy will prove harder than expected and what looks impossible will prove quite feasible. The ridge looked easy.

It was very broken and required constant care. It was the hottest time of the day and instead of dropping to the clear-winding Agoundis I was tackling a world of exposed rock and dirty snow. Every snow band oozed (the ground was frequently mud) but there was never a stream for a drink. I filled my hat with snow and enjoyed the trickle of wet down my face. Eventually the easy ridge ran up in a series of edges and steps. I crawled into the shade of a leaning pinnacle, its overhang giving the first such for many hours. I ate a little and drank a little, hoarding the precious orange juice I'd brought.

The next part was enjoyable as the ridge became narrow and exposed, then suddenly there was a dome of ablated snow—and a cairn—which was celebrated with a mouthful of precious liquid. Being short of water, it became the paramount thought of course.

The descent was over a mixture of snow slope and crag. Rock fell to bits like slush and snow proved rock hard to start with yet, all too soon, the snow was like porridge. The long ridge which demarcated the Agoundis led on in a brown succession of swelling waves. Much of it I traversed below the crest on the drier, southern slopes. Occasional juniper trees dotted the landscape.

The Agoundis flank remained excessively steep, precipitous or snow-bound. A ski stick is not quite a substitute for an ice axe and crampons. I was becoming very dehydrated and tired. My last liquid was consumed long before the end hump, which was also the highest. I had a long rest. From there I looked across the Agoundis to the Tazharhart plateau from which we had descended to the Agoundis last time. Mine had been an aesthetic choice really—the valley would have been a repetition whereas I'd enjoyed a certain novelty.

Tigoundafine village lay below in edging shadows. We had been royally entertained there, enjoyed the traditional mint tea and a *cous cous* made of the bunny which was hopping about our feet when we arrived. Our room for the night was like a furnace and it also produced swarms of biting creatures: long or round, the two species were both hairy, relished wallowing in DDT powder and even supplied an airborne division to drop on us from the rafters.

There is a very definite, fortunately indescribable smell from slaughtered bugs. I vowed never to sleep indoors in the Agoundis again.

Not that I now could. I was still high above all life. I sloped off towards little valleys, mere bellyfolds among the flanks of my hill hoping to find water and a bivy site. Suddenly I heard sheep and goats and sure enough a pixy-like figure in *djellaba* was racing across the rocks. I quickly placed my ski stick on my shady side (it glitters in the sun) and dropped behind a scarp. The Berbers are marvellously hospitable, but . . . I'd prefer to bivouac!

Several gullies had been dry but eventually I found a trickle below some wet ground I placed my bottle under a dribbly rock and then drank half a litre in one go. While it filled again I scooped out a pool for later. I soaked apple flakes in a poly bag then started a small scrub fire. Two junipers yielded dead twigs enough and I stockpiled for the morning too. The blessed bulk of that meal was a litre or three of sweet, milky, British char.

The slopes burned orange in the last of the sun, and just as flames die, the colours seemed to waver out into nightfall. A bright yellow star in the west, Orion above, one that winked brilliantly in the east, the Seven Sisters . . . I lay back in delicious content while the blanket of the dark patched itself with stars. Northerners never see stars like that. People refer to the desert as dead but few places give such a palette of unmixed colours by day or such an extravagance of stars by night. But this opulence and extravagance of the desert is only given to those who shrive themselves and walk gently.

A clatter of stones and raucous voices jolted me out of dusk dreams. Two lads were driving an unwilling mule along a path far below. The whole pantomime was vocal and slowly moved off across the slopes. "Hirra! Hirra!—the cajoling cry echoed and died. When they had gone it was dark, but, slowly, subtly, the starlight grew till it was possible to arrange things a bit. Damart thermawear next to the skin, *duvet*, and lower half inside the extended rucksack was my scheme of bedding. It was not really adequate. The water in my bottle froze overnight.

Under these circumstances I was very aware of the stars' slow perambulation. During the one longer spell of sleep the Plough swung up over the ridge and was suddenly there when cramp and shivering woke me. I look to the north as a good Moslem looks to Mecca. For the rest of the night I watched the Plough, and knew where home lay.

An hour before day I relit my tiny fire. All my evening's tea had been absorbed, which showed my drouthy state. I had another litre for breakfast and some *muesli* which had soaked overnight. Soaked? Part soaked, then frozen. I heated it too.

If sunset is memorable, then sunrise is unforgettable. The snows on the slopes opposite caught the first light, and for the next two or three hours the sun-line on the hillside chased me down, down into the depths of the Agoundis, then the sun swept overhead and for the

Trekking in Morocco's High Atlas Mountains

rest of the day there was no escape. If you travel deserts, sunset is bliss, and sunrise a call to hasten the journey.

It must have been 3,000 feet down a side valley to the Agoundis itself. Two women were toiling up a slope above the highest village when I suddenly came on them. They stopped in amazement. An elderly man, wrinkled and wrapped in many layers of garments, drew himself up and greeted me with dignity:

"Las bas!"

"La bas!" I replied.

Beyond that high village I hit the first path I'd had and the feeling of remoteness vanished. It was still an environment as harsh as any but it was peopled. I rounded a corner and stood on a prow a thousand feet above the river.

The eye looked down on stepped terraces of incredible green. Here and there almond blossom seemed to explode, carelessly as children's fireworks, many-tinted. The river had been led off in *seguias* and tumbled below a village in a braided fall. Above water-level all was barren. Sun-blasted rock. Paradise is merely water.

I dropped to the river (clear and covering a treasure-chest of coloured pebbles) and took the path up to the village (it was also a water-course, refuse dump, loo and hen-run).

The next few hours simply fuse now in one long memory of delight. The Agoundis is very steep-sided, often precipitous, with churning gorges, so deep that only up side glens could one glimpse the snows which had been my world the day before. Strung along at regular intervals (wherever there was water flowing from the rock) were mud-built villages. They were prosperous and only insolence or ignorance would view the people with condescension. They are well aware of the beauty. The cool interiors may be spread with carpets while through the grilled wrought-iron windows would be a view of unqualified beauty.

You kick off your shoes on entering the guest room. (Only filthy Westerners take their dirty shoes into their homes.) You sprawl comfortably while the head of the house prepares mint tea: sweet and piquant. You drink it piping hot from little glasses.

Walnuts are often produced with the tea. Time means little and social graces have not been lost—yet. The lowest common denominator of Western civilisation is creeping up here though. You can judge it by the tidal litter of indestructable plastic. Some day we will all be the same by greed, not decree, by ease, not labour. There will be no point going to the Agoundis then.

Village followed village, each romantically built up on rocky buttresses. No arable patch is built on: the houses are perched above *seguias* and water level. After all the water can be carried up in great jars every day. What else are women for?

Women were much more in evidence than men. I think I only met half a dozen men all down the valley. One was planing wood in a courtyard, another greeted me with a torrent of meaningless words from his rooftop and a child tapped his head and nodded at the wild fellow, another was doing a Christopher Robin act, rushing up and down a *seguia* in his wellington boots, desperately trying to stop water overflowing its banks. Though all goods must be carried by mule or donkey I met no beasts at all. The path followed a line which took it happily through cliff and crag, up stairs and down, a dizzy progression that, at times, required a head for heights for the pedestrian. I have a soft spot for donkeys.

The colours were breathtaking: the close-knitted fields, some no bigger that a table top, edged with iris, and over all the dazzle of almond. The slight breeze occasionally blew their pink and white confetti about my head. It was full spring at this level. A dipper in the burn, a robin in the garden, the hammer of a woodpecker, blackbird and chaffinch and warbler songs—it could have been rural England. But we don't see martins or lesser kestrels up on the February crags, nor a sailing lammergeyer, nor the *teebeebit* (house bunting—which replaces our sparrow), nor bulbuls diving among the shrubbery. On the barren slopes the vivid Moussier's redstart and crimson-winged finch very definately say it is Africa.

The women wore brilliant pinks and greens while layers of iridescent cloth alternated with flowing muslin. Round their heads they wore colourful scarves. On their feet—green plastic sandals.

The houses are intricately built one on top of the other. Like Swiss peasants the people live above their cattle for warmth (scented central heating). The rooms are ranged round so that they look out on a rooftop. Possessions are few. Nobody seems to be very busy yet on every side there is the evidence of great labour. Both work and leisure are dignified still.

The valley began to open up: ilex, juniper, *thuyas,* palm trees, almonds crowded the slopes, prickly pears grew on the cliffs. The villages became larger, the *seguias* deeper. Ahead I could see a modern road zig-zagging up the hillside in unnatural symmetry and suddenly I was looking down on European houses and the tin buildings of a mine. Cars glittered outside the office block and the bang-bang of machinery broke the spell of the hours past.

I walked down about another seven or eight miles before a noon stop to soak feet in a *seguia.* The motor track was harsher by far than the stony donkey path. I had a picnic. Crested larks and rock buntings darted along the banks. A flock of over a hundred alpine choughs swung and cackled its way opposite. The sun blazed down. I washed my floppy hat and put it on. In ten minutes it was dry. I was content, though, for the Agoundis lay behind, safely gathered, like some harvest, into a store of special memories.

I walked the last mile or two down to Ijoukak. I went into a cafe for a drink and sat happily, half asleep, looking out of its cool darkness. A stall across the road was doing a flourishing trade in doughnuts. An old, blind beggar tapped his way up the street only to be bustled aside as a big tourist car rushed through.

"Many tourists. Souk at Kasbah Tadla. Three kilometres."

That sounded hopeful, for no amount of asking could elucidate a bus time. There are only two roads over the Atlas and both lead to big towns of ringing names: Taroudant and Ourzazate (Ou is pronounced W). Perhaps I could wander on and either get a lift or a bus in due course.

Which is what happened, but "due course" was three hours and ten miles of desert grilling later. It was staggeringly hot. I was out of water and apart from the main stream there was no trickle. It was the Oued Nfis now anyway, having swallowed up the Agoundis at Ijoukak. I had one pause in those scorching hours and sat under some stunted olives with a view of the road. A shepherd lad was playing his pipe up the shimmering slope above. I ate the last of my sweaty cheese and ten-day-old bread. I thumbed anything and everything. A Volkswagon van the size and colour of my dormobile passed. I counted 15 folk inside and it was piled high on top with boxes and three unhappy sheep. I thumbed it.

A few miles on I thumbed an oil tanker—and it stopped. The wee walk was over. We sped for the fleshpots of Marrakech.

Kipling has one odd contact with the Atlas. His story "The Man Who Would Be King" was filmed there. This tale of rascals who set off over the North-west Frontier to become kings takes our dreams to their most fanciful conclusion; but IF, just IF I could be king, I think I would be king of the Agoundis.

24. Iceland alive

IT was on the seventh day we descended into Hell; a slippery slope indeed but leading to a soothing warmth rather than any roasting.

This Hell (Viti) was a volcanic, sulphurous lake, pancake-round, a deep-set crater in the vast Askja *caldera*. It was an explosion crater we were informed, produced in one big bang, as against a steady lava-producing rent in the earth. No, the smelly steam vents on its slopes were quite harmless. The most recent activity was that lava flow over there. It was about ten years old. Some of the lavas we had come through were much younger than that.

I plastered the talcum-smooth mud over my neck, relishing the oddity of the situation. At home it is many millions of years since our rocks were bared to view. Here we were seeing creation, raw from the crucible, nature very naked indeed. Perhaps it was apt that our gang, of all ages and several nationalities, had stripped of clothes (and any inhibitions) for that vitalising dip in Viti. It was symbolic of many things.

It was perhaps symbolic of Iceland itself. Here we were, this mixed bag from the ends of the earth, bathing in an almost inaccessible geothermal area in the heart of the last sizeable country to be inhabited by man. Being there was testimony to the resilience of mankind, for Iceland is explosively tough, yet enjoys much of the good life. They have learnt to live with nature in a way we have long forgotten. It is the landscape that makes Iceland memorable, the additional human elements make it enjoyable.

To the British visitor the two main drawbacks of the country are its weather (which tends to be on the bleaker-side of Scottish) and the high cost of everything—prices are at least twice, perhaps three times, those at home. In the youth hostel at Reykjavik I watched a student place a loaf of bread on the table. "One pound," he smiled wryly. A tin of beans followed: "One pound." Three apples: "One pound." He no longer smiled.

Having read the small print I was aware of this financial ambush. I had brought supplies from home to see me through the odd days in the capital that topped and tailed the "Highland Walking Safari" I went on as being the best way of seeing many of the best sites and

Iceland—land of fire and water. The powerful flow of Gullfoss

also of using the legs—without having to spend a fortune as an independent traveller. For a completely new continent, or a country with marked differences, going on an organised party can be an economically wise survey as well as a holiday in its own right. After all, the biggest insult you can pay a country is to visit it only once.

Iceland has a population about the same as Aberdeen and half the number live in or around the capital. Reykjavik. The rest are scattered on the green fringes, about 7 per cent of the country, which leaves a vast amount of emptiness. Some of this is indeed ice (the Vatnajokull is the largest ice cap in Europe) but it is also black desert and technicoloured desert, it is also water (shooting up in geysers or thundering in astonishing falls), and it is fire, an aspect which is not easily forgotten.

Our "tour" was organised by a firm with the resonant name of Ulfar Jacobsen. (Mytton and Oswin, 164 Upper New Walk, Leicester LE1 7QF are one British agent for this and many other tours.) I was a bit horrified to find we were two bus-loads travelling together but as the second bus's passengers were mostly French and German it added interest. Along with the buses went a mobile kitchen and during the day it would travel ahead so we arrived to food cooked and ready.

Mutton and fish alternated throughout! There was plenty to eat. The only item that met with some suspicion was the sweet soup. That came on alternative days too. Two teenage girls and a lad prepared the meals. All children over thirteen *have* to work for six weeks of their long summer break. All the vehicles had high clearance, four-wheeled drive and other tough additions to cope with the dirt roads of the country.

Our days also seemed to alternate: long drives, and moderate walking, with most camp sites used for two nights at a time. The firm provided sturdy tents accommodating two people and sleeping bags if required. Considering the wide range of experience (or lack of it) camp would spring up surprisingly quickly. Perhaps the supper queue had something to do with it.

A few people were shocked at the primitiveness and at the occasional bitter weather. I became quite friendly with one overweight woman from Nîmes who was quite out of her depth but quite irrepressible. Pitching a tent was not her métier, but she added words to my invocative vocabulary.

Our first day's drive took us round the coast and then inland to Thingvellir, the site of Iceland's original parliament a thousand years ago. The people are fiercely democratic and patriotic, deeply grounded in their history (unlike Scots) yet they have never fought a real war and have no armed forces. Unemployment is under 1 per cent and when the long arctic night becomes the longer arctic summer construction work goes at a frantic pace.

Hence the school workforce. Everyone works, without demarcations or disputes. To balance this work-mania every other Icelander seems to be a poet. At Thingvellir a plot was laid out 20 years ago to become a national cemetery. So far it has been used for two poets— and no politicians.

At Thingvellir, over lunchtime, I spotted two black-tailed godwits while several phalaropes landed a few yards away and an arctic skua flew past. Whimbrels called. This was to be a familiar pattern: the rarities of North Britain being the common birds of Iceland. If you saw a thrush it had to be a redwing, their only *turdus* species. Their species list is short but thrilling.

The flowers followed the same pattern and while Londoners or lowland continentals could hardly recognise anything, the Scottish hill-walkers felt uneasily at home; uneasy, because of the abundance (moss campion might, one day, fill a plain rather that being a doll's cushion rarity on the Fannichs). On the last day we drove over the black ash desert below Hekla. A year after the eruption the first stars of grass are appearing and in a shady cranny there was a campion, a starry saxifrage and Silene. There were also sheep grazing—we are not the only wooly destroyers!

That day we also visited Gullfoss, perhaps the most beautiful fall in the country. It was only saved from the doom of hydro development by hard fighting. Developers are no more sensitive in Iceland than at home. Iceland has recently expanded her hydro works, at the price of big debts to pay for it, but most homes now have electricity, that boon which is so easily taken for granted. Experiments with geothermal power are not going so well but hot water, tapped from the earth, provides all the heating (and on-tap hot water) for most towns. Our campsite that night, at Geysir, could not produce *cold* water!

Geyser has entered all languages and from the camp site we looked up to the periodic spectacle of an explosion of boiling water erupting into the air. This was a geyser called Strokkur, for Geysir itself can only be persuaded to work nowadays by pouring several hundredweight of soap powder into its vent. There were also pots of boiling mud and one still pool of delicate turquoise blue. One vent is tapped and its heat used to warm greenhouses. They grow bananas in Iceland!

At Myvatn later we saw similar areas. It is highly unsettled and one farmer, on lifting his potatoes, found they had been cooked. A favourite cavern, used as the local swimming pool, had to be abandoned when the temperature shot up. We saw another thermal area in the middle of our crossing the island next day: a *hot* oasis in a bleak area of arctic desert and ice caps. A snow bunting sitting by a hot spring was distinctly odd.

The north of Iceland enjoys better weather and has most of the richer agricultural ground. A ring road now circuits the island. Across the centre lie deserts and ice caps, mountains and rivers, which makes it very hard to cross. Hence our buses built like tanks. We made the crossing twice: going by the Kjölur (Keel) pass and returning by the Sprengisandur. Both have legends and stories. They make the Lairig Ghru seem a Sunday afternoon stroll. We went along the north and then turned south to penetrate to Askja, the huge *caldera* mentioned at the start. We camped at a site which was surrounded by miles of jagged lavas.

The road through was a nightmare: it was quicker to walk. The green oasis was the more welcome for the contrast but at it we had our own minor drama. The site can only be reached by fording a river, which bounds the site and has another river entering it there. This river suddenly began to rise. We evacuated the site and moved to higher ground. Several rough-stuff cars were marooned at the ford (now a lake) and our big buses went off to rescue the occupants. They were put up in a refuge hut. The torrent went down overnight and they then rescued the cars.

Our worst site proved to be the last. It came at the end of a thirteen-hour crossing of the central wilderness, by the Sprengisandur route. A short-cut ended at a snow drift across the road. Mountains of every shade gloomed out of the mist. It rained. It was cold. Our guide warned us the site was miserable but that there were hot springs to relax in. Being a bit of a joker we did not believe him. We had seen postcards with lush green meadows in front of tents.

The lush green turned out to be waterlogged moss, not grass, and we arrived with two other "tours" so something like eighty tents were being pitched simultaneously on a surface that, at its politest, was referred to as "lunar". The old bird from Nîmes was "doing a Monsieur Hulot." She would raise one end of the tent and as soon as the other end was lifted the first would collapse. Pegs would not go in. It was not a silent pantomime, however.

I helped her out, produced a cup of coffee and fetched her suitcase. "Très gentil!" I was called. The beaten ground where the kitchen stood was waterlogged so you could not sit to eat. Landmannalaugar was much too like the Clachaig in November. The hot springs were good. I'm told a bottle of duty free whisky led to a late night for some bathers. (Alcohol sales are strictly controlled by the Government.)

That last day allowed local walking and also a look at Ofaerufoss, a big double cascade with a natural arch spanning it. Iceland is, as no other country I know, the land of waterfalls. Both Iceland and Scotland may have had the driest summer in years but this is balanced in Iceland by river sources being up in icefields where more sun simply meant more melting. We were not to suffer the three usual detractions of Scotland: mobs, midges and a monsoon.

We could have met the last two certainly but even Lake Myvatn (which means Lake of Midges) was kind to us and our visit coincided with the week's pause between the two breeding generations that plague the summer. The dead midges round the loch make a good fertiliser! I'm not joking: they are rich in nitrogen, which plants need. The grazing there is lush. I saw one cow swathed in a harness of some kind and, on asking what this was, was told it was a sort of truss to help support her bulging sack of milk. A cow wearing a bra!

Iceland is no Shangri-La. Inflation was running at 100 per cent recently—but was then tackled in a fashion that reduced it to single figures in a year. This element of knuckling-down to dealing with problems is something we seem to lack but then Scotland has lost that vital driving-force of national pride.

The Icelander has tremendous pride in himself, in his work, in his country. They have learnt to live, and prosper, in an unforgiving environment. Perhaps our world would be less likely to erupt if our leaders were packed off to live in the wilds of Iceland (or even Scotland) for a while. Could you imagine Maggie Thatcher and Arthur Scargill stripping off for a sulphurous bath in Hell together?

25. Under Cezanne's mountain

THE south of France has a reputation for sunshine as meaningless as Skye's for rain. My visits have, to be fair, usually been made early in the year. It is only later the Van Gogh sun shines and his crows wing across golden cornfields.

On my first visit, Mont St Victoire hid in a West Highland mist and the rain rushed down the gutters in a red flow. The next time I went to its summit (mentioned in one of Scott's novels) and slept out in the maquis for half a night before the rain came on and I had to descend through a hole in the mountain and huddle in a draughty corner.

Aix-en-Provence is the capital of this largely-forgotten hinterland, a lively town of music festivals, Moroccan ghettos, and French cooking at its best—reward enough for a night on the bare limestone mountain that Cezanne drew scores of times in every light and style.

We returned to its slopes to sleep in the handy camping car, supper rounded off with a local wine, and the smell of coffee not quite overcoming that of the pines and the cistus flowers.

The landscape is familiar from painting. The vivid flatness towards the Camargue, the spurs of dark cypress trees, the ancient towns with names like Arles, Saintes Maries-de-la-Mer, Aigues-Mortes—these Van Gogh had dashed down with demented insight, smitten by the sun and addicted. Chagall, Bonnard, Leger, Matisse, Dufy and Picasso (for his last long years) all came to Provence.

Provence is a vast plain through which the Rhône flows, but it is broken up by hill ranges: the Alpilles, Mont Ventoux, le Massif de la Sainte Baume, the last being one of the country's finest forests, old as time, for the Romans wrote of fearsome ghosts and abominable human sacrifices of children in its glades and grottos.

The affluent, modernistic, developments I think look appalling in these areas: ski resorts which have slipped to the sea. For those who like wine, women and song, all loudly amplified, then it is a sort of plastic paradise.

Provence, once you are away from the frantic coast, is seemingly full of Roman remains. In Orange the road has to circle round a grand triumphal arch, in Nîmes and Arles there are arenas to rival the Colisseum and at dusk one day we drove in to a camp site at Pont du Gard to find it cringing under the spans of a huge aquaduct. This was so strongly built that it now carries modern road traffic and not just water. The arenas may no longer put on gladiators but the proximity of Spain has created a bull-fighting tradition.

It is not all Roman. There is still Avignon of the Popes with the bridge of the song—though this is so narrow you could not even manage an eightsome reel on it; there is Tarascon, the magnificent castle of good King René, 13th century but so immaculate it looks as if made of Lego bricks; there is the Abbey of Montmajour, which was closed down in 1786 following a scandel involving the Cardinal Abbot and was sold off to a female junk dealer on credit which she tried to repay by ripping it down and selling it bit by bit. The creditors moved in before she ruined it. A film company were using it for location work when we called.

The name that made me pause to wonder in Provence, rather than just rush through, was Les Baux. It is a fortified town perched on rock like Edinburgh Castle and as a kid I had been fascinated by aerial plans of the town and its gory history.

Mistrel (Provence's equivalent of Scott and Burns) described the seigneurs of Les Baux as "the eagle race who were never vassals." They were a race of proud, vicious thugs as far as I can see, even if descended from Balthazar, one of the three kings of the Christmas story.

The village remains and you can peer out of a sitting room window down six hundred feet to the fields below. Baux gave its name to bauxite just as Strontian did to strontium.

"Modern" history began with the Greeks establishing Marseilles for commercial exploration. The western Iberians and the eastern Ligurians resented this intrusion, so appealed to the Romans, who settled the argument by moving in themselves and creating "Provincia Romana"—hence Provence.

Hannibal with his elephants crossed the hills, England's Richard the Lionheart once held the fief of Provence and, from Orange, a family moved up in the world to gain what is now Holland, then crossed the channel to Britain.

As a climber, I have a sneaking affection for the early poet Petrach for, in 1336, he climbed Mont Ventoux, the highest peak in

Cezanne Country, Provence, the fine castle at Tarascon

Provence, which is the earliest recorded alpine scent made purely for pleasure.

The people have remained sturdily uncentralised and effervescent. Heading for Marseilles and the ferry to Morocco last time we had a fairly typical incident. It was raining hard, of course. The car in front of me tooted at the one in front of him as he considered it was going too slowly. It promptly slowed down! It was given another toot. So slowed down again. So toot again. After a few minutes of this irate "conversation" the leading car stopped and the driver walked back to tell the impatient one a thing or two.

Number two jumped out and a voluble argument began. Others began to blow their horns at the pair till the din was frightful. They could not even hear themselves argue, so suddenly joined forces to storm back at the rest of the world. Being the next car I took the first assault! Immediately the driver behind me leapt out to my rescue. Did they not see my "Ecosse" plate? What way was that to treat a visitor to Provence. Tremendous apologies were then made all round, the original culprits edged their cars forward so I could ease out and away, but as I drove off I noticed in my mirror they had returned to the fray and I went off in a fading cacophony of horn-blowing.

DOUBTS AND RESERVATIONS

Sometimes happiness can be left gasping for breath.
Sometimes it is time to cry out in protest. So far I have
tried to keep my doubts and sorrows in check but before
my pilgrim band of readers leaves the hills and the sea I
would ask you to look again at the Promised Land. Can
you really see it clearly—or are there clouds over some of
the slopes we tread?

26. Blots on the landscape

THERE is a beautiful glen in the North and its whisky-coloured falls and peat-black pools are crowded with golden-leaved rowans, red-berried at this time of year: a flame of brightness among the staid alders and stiff pines. I had humped my pack a mile or two to reach it and I held back from the camp site round the bend simply to increase the emotions of expectancy. Memory had it as a listed site: treasured, sparkling and clean.

The walk up from the road was a sair pech but rewarded by a constant coming and going of little birds. A party of long-tailed tits came first, like flying teaspoons and they swarmed all over a solitary birch then, in ones and threes, drifted off down the burn. A buzzard mewed up on the invisible bee-loud heather moor where the broch ruins lie, heard but not seen as we followed the deep vee of the burn. A raven croaked, also out of sight, and the trees ahead seemed to sizzle with sound. I was compiling quite a bird list for the day.

The dog and I pulled up to sit on a level with the tops of the trees, a mix of shivery birch, alder and scrubby, scruffy, willow. There was a wee breeze so we did not have to endure a craze of midges. We sat quiet and soon were watching four great tits—noisy big brutes they seemed beside a solitary feather-faded blue tit and a pair of hyperactive goldcrest. The scrub erupted with shouting wrens.

A keeper friend always used to refer to wrens as "noisy little buggers" but he also used the same expression about the romping puppies his bitch collie had produced and of his and the neighbouring kids (the entire school population of seven) as they played cowboys and indians in the bracken. Wrens are just like that.

I was quite glad to be moving again after this listing of busy birds for I had grown stiff and Storm, the dog, had yawned rather pointedly a few times. So we scrambled on, revelling in the clean, sharp air of autumn.

There were still tiny sundews scattered on the moss banks and the nodding heads of scabious skied blue over the heather. The spikes of asphodel had lost their gold but St John's wort provided the yellow with which nature paints so extravagantly. The banks were deep with the dead leaves of primrose, that flower of spring. I seemed to be listing flowers too without actually doing it consciously. Perhaps listing is not the right word. Nor is recording. It was an absorption, a natural acceptance, a meeting of expected things in their proper place. Rarities may startle but the old friends are the good companions. A million years had gone to give our moments of delight. You walk humbly up a Highland burn.

As I paused for a last breather before the secret place where we planned to camp I remembered "last time" when we came on it, dog and I, at the end of a long hot day, the seventh in a row as we tramped Scotland coast-to-coast. It was rough, tough, heathery country, calling for guile and patience rather than brute slogging. I like camping by a burn. It is a cheery last and first sound with which to surround good sleep. Thus when we came on the deep vee we looked for a site. As soon as we had sloped down a deer track into the glen we found the spot—the seventh good one in a row. I've a huge list of such secret sites.

It was a machair-like lawn of tight grass, starred with eye-bright and tormentil and edged with bedstraw and thyme—presumably the result of gravels washed down in some historic spate and left as an enriched bank among the acid soils. The burn curved round it on three sides and you could perhaps have squeezed three tents onto its mattress of green. It was a delectable site.

On that journey the dog and I had been woken the next morning by the click-clicking of something coming down the track. The dog sniffed and knew but I had to peer out the ventilator to see three stags (in velvet) coming down. They actually stepped over the rear guyline. I was glad our intrusion had not scared them. Just "being there" can have its rewards.

I was once sitting with my previous dog, Kitchy, in a wood near

Birnam, leaning against a big beach with my legs out across an animal track. A squirrel came rushing along, its mind obviously elsewhere, for it just did not see my legs and went crashing over them. He picked himself up swearing like a trooper—which may be a cliché but was certainly not anthropomorphic. The dog turned and gave me a prim look which sent me into hoots of laughter.

Before we even had the dixie on for the first brew during the crossing stay we had another pleasure to list. A dipper was busy in the burn ten yards away. She kept rushing into the water (like an excited bather) and scurrying along the bottom. I could see the glitter of bubbles on her back. She would bob out again, curtsey a few times, and then flit back to Go.

You can see why I had to pause before rounding the corner to this site again.

"Come on dog!" I urged Storm.

We climbed round by a lichened, mossy crag and stopped, stunned and horrified. Now, if another flash flood had simply obliterated the site, this would have been accepted as part of nature, as much as a bonxie drowning and plucking a puffin, or a noble Scots pine being smashed by lightening. That sort of thing is in the natural order. What we met was not, and the list I then made was one compiled in cold rage against the vilest predator of all.

Here is my list:

Item: one bonfire site which had destroyed a square yard right in the middle of the "lawn" and whose boulders held a paste of charcoal, silver paper and melted plastic.

Item: eight boulders (besides the fireplace ones) each of which, when I'd thrown them back in the burn, left a scar which will need two seasons to heal.

Item: three dead patches of grass where a hot pan had been put down or boiling water poured out. That damage will take several years to vanish.

Item: six tins, various, which had been tossed into the burn; and four more tins on the grass.

Item: an uncounted scattering of plastic cups, paper plates, paper wrappers, sweet papers, orange coloured serviettes and such litter.

Item: One hairpin, one length of plastic string, one revolting hanky,

ten ring-pulls from cans, 17 fag-ends and 26 used matches.
Item: one dead posy of assorted wild flowers, picked and abandoned.
Item: seven beer and/or coke cans.
Item: one whisky bottle, one sherry bottle and two lemonade bottles, all in scattered smitherscreens after being set up and stoned. (My hour-long clean-up was interrupted to deal with a cut on Storm's paw from the broken glass and I wondered how many deer had crossed by their ford to be cut in like manner).

There was no doubt more but I gave up after a bit. I'm really not very good at listing things, not even the birds and flowers that are the decorative icing on the rich cake of wilderness content. My list of the objectionable in the wilds is minute. It only contains one species: *Homo sapiens.*

27. Losing the Unna Vision

SCOTLAND'S unique wilderness has been suffering a succession of acts of official vandalism over the last few years and a growing number of people who love the wilds are becoming both alarmed and angry.

The alarm is caused by the wild escalation in the number of projects which are endangering the very character of Scottish hillgoing. The damage is caused by the blatant disregard for all the traditions and the undemocratic way the soviets of public bodies behave.

The defensive cry, of course, is that we are being elitist and selfish. If elitism is wanting good rather than bad and best rather than better, we are elitist. If wanting to preserve our hill quality and traditions free of man-made junk is selfish, we are selfish. The sad thing about the Countryside Commission's West Highland Way or the opencast NTS use of mountain landscapes is in their limited vision.

Men who sit in offices are telling the outdoor users where to go and what to do. The result is a demeaning, if not a destruction, of the wild quality which has made Scotland different. It is no doubt wellintended. So was thalidomide.

The argument is often put forward that by attracting people to NTS mountain properties other areas are saved. This is a fallacy. You do not sacrifice the superlative for the second best. The NTS were given these areas because of their quality and they were given to be protected, to be kept in their primitive state, freely accessible, but undeveloped. The NTS have clearly and determinedly built and developed—a shocking conceit, for it implies Percy Unna did not know what he meant.

The same dangers lurked in the Lurchers affair that smoke-screen name, for at risk really was Coire an Lochain,, one of Britain's finest scenic places, which could be destroyed for the ocasional selfish needs of weekend skiers. It is disgraceful that after generations of talk, committees and reports the Government have not ensured that such areas are made sacrosanct. Any outstanding area can be destroyed for the controls are minimal. (Yet you try to build a garage without permission!) The bulldozed mountain tracks were typical.

211

I am not knocking the NTS. I think they do much splendid work and have saved much that is valuable in our heritage, but with their very different mountain properties they seem to be out of their depth and their policies are proving destructive. These lands were taken on with the very clear "Unna Rules" as a guide. The NTS keep saying they believe they are following Unna's ideas—but this you can judge for yourself. Perhaps some day stronger judgments will be needed for the NTS have no intention of moderating their Wimpey-Trust House Forte approach.

There are plenty of mountain users in the NTS membership but whenever people like Dr Adam Watson or I dare breathe any criticism we are simply howled down. Help is not wanted. The NTS "mountain consultant," the eminent W.H. Murray, is in fact seldom consulted. Recently the executive have thrown out a report on the benefits of having an advisory committee on mountains.

The NTS executive or council have limited mountain knowledge. Unna's expertise counts for nothing. When they had hopes of taking over Rhum (the only genuine Nature Conservancy Council owned and managed wilderness) it was with the avowed intention of maximum development. If this is not a perversion of mountain policy then words have no meaning.

Percy Unna was a keen member of the Scottish Mountaineering Club and largely through his generosity most of the NTS mountain properties were purchased for the public. As president of the club he wrote to the Chairman and Council of the NTS, on behalf of all who had subscribed, as "it is desirable that what are believed to be the views of the subscribers as to the future of the estate (Dalness) should be expressed in writing, and recorded in the Minutes of the Trust ... the Trust be asked to undertake that the land be maintained in its primitive condition for all time with unrestricted access to the public." Points are then spelt out, which I give, sightly abridged:

1. Primitive means not less primitive than the existing state.

2. Grazing may continue but not stalking as this could interfere with free access and use. Deer would still need culling.

3. Regulations are not excluded but, if any, only if absolutely necessary, and in sympathy with the views expressed herein.

4. Hills not to be made easier or safer.

The Sound of Sleat looking across to the peaks of Knoydart

5.   No mechanical transport allowed, no extending or improving paths, or making new ones.

6.   No signposts, paint marks, cairns etc. allowed, other than to show NTS ownership.

7.   A demand for hotels or hostels might need satisfying to a small extent (climbers in Glencoe the inference) but nothing to be built in Glencoe itself. Neighbouring estates to be encouraged to follow a similar policy.

8.   No other facilities for lodging, shelter, food or drink and especially no shelter of any kind on the hills.

9.   Careful consideration to any building design and screening by trees.

10.   Management to receive special attention as it could be a precedent for other mountain areas, in Scotland and elsewhere.

We have failed Unna dismally and far from setting an example Scotland now apes procedures from south of the Border. The setting up of official "Ways" is a case in point. Vast repair work is now needed on some Ways in England. With a hundred "Ways" nobody could walk them all in a lifetime. Scotland had a chance to remain free of them but we threw it away. The qualities that make Scotland different, and attractive, and loved, are being lost.

Even in little things we seem to have no logic. Some of the hardest fighters against a bridge at Corruisk in Skye spent a happy time building one in Knoydart with all the secrecy of conniving bureaucracy. In the last decade every glen west to the sea has had the foul intrusion of greedy man, ranging from insensitive plantings to a line of pylons marching to Skye on a line chosen "because there was nothing there"—not a bad description of wilderness.

Unna was not against people. Their free access was both his concern, and is mine, The NTS policy of grabbing the public and encouraging maximum visitor use is another thing. It is self-defeating. Every development needs more development to pay for development and so on.

Unna's way would have cost next to nothing (a cost met by endowment) for doing NOTHING is virtually free. Even now, if roadside parking was made impossible through Glencoe or over Lawers nature could win back what man has destroyed.

Climbers would howl at this of course, just as way-walkers or skiers at some other comments, and it would do NTS visitor statistics no good. But Unna was not interested in sectarian claims. How valid his concern we see now with the NTS car park horror built right in the heart of Glencoe. The NTS bridged the river and created erosion problems, so the duckboards go down. Pictures of this aspect on Lawyers in the last *Newsletter* finally roused my ire. It was so self-congratulatory, whereas in reality it is a travesty of all Unna hoped for.

This upside-down thinking by our supposedly preservation bodies makes me despair. In my lifetime I am seeing the wild removed from wilderness. I can see no hope for our heritage. If the Countryside Commission for Scotland can go bashing pedestrian motorways through the land, if the NTS can desecrate many of our finest hills, if the mountaineering clubs are so feckless in defence, if the public itself simply does not care, there can be no hope, and our children's children will know nothing of the magic that once was in the hills of Scotland.

Originally I thought of leaving out any controversial pieces but when I re-read the above (written in 1981) I was struck with how little attitudes have changed. It needs saying still—so let it stand. The bungling and duplicity of Government (national and local), of quick-buck landowners and pimping developers is an endemic problem. A list of just some of the ill-conceived projects since I wrote the above is horrific: Craigroyston, Lurchers, Creag Mheagaidh, Knoydart, Glas Maol Wyvis, Grudie-Talladale, Duich Moss . . . while Sutherland is being swamped with conifers, Galloway reccied for dumping nuclear waste, our air and seas polluted by chemicals, and scores of miles of ELF transmitters are waiting to gobble up our hills. We are no longer seeing duck-nibbling changes but an escalating assault. I am not against developments, reasonable and benefiting local people, but people and the land itself are only viewed as assets to be bought and sold at will. Our system of immoral land ownership threatens the rape of the lot. This is delivering into politics which of course conser-

vations are loathe to do—but until we do the present chaos, frustration and impotence under Big Brother (Sister?) will continue. As a third class colonial country allowing itself to be asset-stripped of its heritage perhaps we deserve no better.

One body very aware of the problems and trying to do something about it is the Scottish Wild Land Group. Information can be obtained from the Secretary and membership is recommended. We need a voice to speak for us. Contact SWLG, St. Ronan's, 93 Queen Street, Alva FK12 5AH.

28. White as Winter

THE grey No-man's Land of late autumn is usually battered with a bombardment of snow in early December, rather as the peewit storms of early May give the last rearguard fight of retreating winter.

I like winter.

I like real winter—when the air has bite in it, when feet squeak on frosted pavements and children whoop in the snow. I think it is a sign of our cosseted society how little joy adults are prepared to find in snow.

Peer at the snowflakes landing on a sleeve next time. Every one is a star. Every one is different among the millions. One of nature's quiet miracles. So come winter! Come with paintings on the windows, with tracery on the willows, come blue-tit bold and sparrow chirpy. Turn Greyfriars Bobby into a white poodle. Set the lawyers quacking duck-footed through the drifts round St. Giles.

Yet, it is just these delights that will set folk girning in their hot-house offices and stuffy cars, huddled like cheepy chicks in an incubator. You come in from the caller air to be hit by a wall of smokey, smelly, overwarm, unrefreshing, second-lung air—a perfect breeding ground for germs—and this is thought to be civilised! Poor deprived urbanites, even having to endure the climate at second-hand.

We seem to be battered with overdoing things; canned music with the volume painfully high, TV sets that are never switched off and which grimly cover any sport, topic or news item into smothering boredom, trains with heating so hot that passengers sit gowping like goldfish.

The shrinking daylight hurries winter on. By Christmas the deepest dark has passed. Light inches back but to gain rewards outdoors still means early rising and late returning to capture the daylight. Winter to me is Hogmanay in Kintail, 3,000 feet up, faces flushed in delayed dawn. Or birling across the Minch under a bruised-plum sky with Suilven stark in the pale east, or simply watching the swans fly in to Duddingston Loch and skiting on their bums on the ice.

I think this overdoing things today is a sign of uncertainty.

Civilisation has lost the way and wobbles to an uncertain future. In a crumbling society everyone is out to grab. The British sin is selfishness. The quick buck beats caring foresight every time.

Recently I came back from touring round Ireland. I crossed from Larne to Stranraer and as I wanted to spend a day on the Moffat hills coming home I was glad to land ahead of the massed juggernauts and speed along death road to reach Dumfries at ten to five, dive into a shop and ask for the vital map.

"Maps are upstairs. But we're just closing." I had to grovel to buy my map. I went in for a needed coffee. The greasy oaf behind the counter scowled, gave me my cup and then stormed round to pull the blinds down. I hurried off to buy food. One butcher had some nice cold meats but grunted "I've cleaned the machine. I'm not serving any cold meats now."

I love the arrival of snow. The day glooms. The world seems to crouch down, watchful, breathless, ready to spring. Skies crayon in unexpected shades of darkness. Then it comes. Lazily at first. Odd flakes quizzing a way to earth and dying at the fatal contact. Then there is a sigh and the full, swirling assault starts, snow on snow, a dazzling dance of Dervish intensity. The roadway cannot eat the flakes quickly enough and soon the whole world is grey-washed. The frantic is stilled. Sounds hide. The sphere knows peace. "Isn't is affy?" is civilisation's response.

I went in to a butcher's in Ireland, only he called himself a "Victualler," which was appetising in itself. The welcome was warm. "You English? . . . Ah, Scottish! . . . Me cousin lives in Glasgow . . . What brings you to the west? . . . Oh, you're a mountainy fellow? . . . Come away through—and, here, try a couple of these tomatoes with your chops. Grow them meself, I do . . ." A curtain drew back to reveal that the business was but half butcher, the other half being given over to pub. (I have even seen a combination of pub and undertaker.) Buying those chops took two hours in the end: memorable hours with marvellous company.

The sun shines. Grey snow leaps into whiteness, that dazzle of brightness beyond all hyperbole. Painters and poets are quite upstaged by it. A blade of grass can shine like a Toledo blade, a garden glitter like fairyland, Arthur's Seat become Chimborozo, wonder be small as a snowy teasle head, big as the whole blue sky.

The beauties of snow; a scene near Newtonmore

No wonder we use the term "white as snow." We use it spiritually and morally too, don't we? Perhaps the state of a nation can be judged by how it regards the whiteness of the snow.

The last two pieces are short stories, it is sometimes a relief to turn to fiction. Five Bird Stories *is a small collection of my stories on bird topics; it is obtainable (£1 and large SAE) from Pettycur Publishing, 21 Carlin Craig, Kinghorn, Fife KY3 9RX.*

29. The boy on the rock

CALLUM stood poised on the rock for a long time. The sun was warm and his golden skin tickled with the drying sea water. He stood as a thousand other boys have done on their thousand secret places. He often stood there, for from the rock he could gaze into the glory of the western sea.

His stance looked out from a tight bay, past skerries that moved the waves of the sea at all times and tides, and away past the big island to the limitless horizon. To the edge of his view the waters were blue, but in the centre, straight out west, the waters were like a burnished thing, dazzling the eyes. Callum's face screwed up against the brilliance and beauty. All dreams look to the West.

The rock was his very own—by right of perpetual usage. Here he gathered mussels at low tide as bait for the fishing; here too he had stabbed a conger eel and felt it writhe and wrap its body up his arm. At high tide he often lay to watch the crabs crawling or the breathing barnacles or the tiny codling that darted about among the wrack and weeds.

The rock divided the bay in two, rising from a beach made of coral and broken shells. Here too were pink cowries which he collected for play-money.

He seldom had friends to play with however, and his brothers were too young to count. The rocky shore shut in the bay and the great rock. It was out of sight of the croft house and out of sound of the waterfall that plunged down through the Scots pines and alders towards the shore, half hidden among the heather-topped boulders and rocks.

He was at home on the hill, Callum. Next year his father would really take him out, for he too wanted to be a keeper. He did not enjoy killing, for he loved animals, but it did not raise issues in his mind. The deer had to be controlled, and if people were willing to spend a fortune

221

on a day's stalking that was their affair. If it were not for that there would be nothing else to keep life clinging to that harsh coast.

Not that he regarded it as harsh.

He loved to stand on the rock in a wild autumn gale. The waves would come surging over the skerries and foam through the mouth of the bay, like live creatures.

How often he had perched on the rock, well wrapped-up in oilskins, his knuckles white and numb with cold and the effort of holding against the hurricane. Sometimes he would catch a wave full in the face and retreat spluttering and insulted. It was a game and he gloried in it with the pure glory of youth.

The second game was when he came of an evening in summer simply to swim in the warm waters. It was only later that the magic of those moments came to mean so much. It was almost the last fling of youth had he known it.

He remembered it so clearly, the lift of his heels from the sharpness of the barnacled rock, the dazzle of the sun in his eyes and the ageless moment suspended in the air before his naked body was swallowed up in the grasp of the green depths.

Down he dived until he could see the weeds and sand and starfish. He rolled like a seal so the bubbles flew about and lazily, slowly, arches back to break the silvered surface.

He emerged laughing and swam for the shore. He stranded himself in the shallows and let the waves break and wash about him. Then with a cry like a wounded sea-bird he sprang to his feet and sprinted along the white sands.

He climbed up the rock and, almost dry, pulled on his shirt and shorts, jumped down and slowly wended his way home by the back path which came out by the kennels.

He was not to return there as a boy again.

★   ★   ★

There were grim faces when he reached home. It was something about war. He had heard of Hitler, of course, but he had had no idea it could or would affect his home.

Two weeks later his father left, and six months later he was dead.

Callum and his brothers and mother went to live with an aunt in Glasgow after that and he grew up among the tenements to the south of the river. He went to the "Tech" and did well enough to settle in a good job and get married.

All through those rough years the memory of his home in the far north-west never dimmed. In the awkward years of adolescence it had been his secret retreat and in National Service (when sweating the years through in Aden) it had always been the cottage by the bay that he had looked to as home.

As a student, too, when money had been tight and the grind hard, it had encouraged him. It gathered to itself almost a sacredness—perhaps because it had been so swift and searing in purity, beauty and freedom, and ever since there had been so much that was petty, sordid and ugly.

Adulthood had an even dullness to it and the memory always produced a sense of guilt that he was such a bound creature, travelling every day to the same office on the same underground with the same company, the same friends, conversations and habits. He hated the numb normality of his city life.

Affluence had recently made Callum mobile, and he and his wife Cynthia, drove north for their brief two weeks annual holiday. He had a secret plan to visit the scene of his childhood, but even his wife did not realise quite what a pilgrimage it was.

They twisted up the road by Loch Lomond in the rain, but two days later, when they had passed Inverness, it had cleared and the following days shone fair. They took the new road by Shieldaig, and Ben Alligin rose like a phantom from an early morning mist to welcome them to the land of youth.

Many hours later he walked almost hesitantly down the hill path towards the bay. The evening sun tumbled its light down the slope before him and the sea vanished into a haze in the golden west.

He had left his wife at the clachan as she had thought it "quaint" and wanted to buy a Shetland cardigan and write postcards to everybody.

He hesitated a second. What if the cottage were a ruin—unlived in all these years. He skirted it by the back path and noticed the kennel railings were rusty and paintless. He took the back path too so as to come suddenly on the rock in the bay.

It was a balmy evening and Callum took off his shoes to go barefoot as he had done as a boy. After stubbing a toe and stepping on a thistle he put his shoes back on. He mopped the sweat off his brow. He had to go through a hole below a boulder and he found it a tight fit. He put one foot in the burn, too, and narrowly missed sitting down in it. For the first time in his life he almost desired normality. In perspiring frustration he questioned the sanity of this ridiculous visit.

"Thank goodness, there's the last corner."

And round it, the rock would soon be in full sight against the western sea. In spite of everything he felt his heart beating quicker. A score of years and more was a long time in any man's days and dreams.

Callum smiled at his adventure, and rounded the corner.

He stopped dead.

A boy stood poised on the rock. He stood with his face screwed up against the brilliance of the sun-bright sea; the silver shimmer of the waves reflected the light so it rimmed the lithe figure with gold.

Callum plainly heard a laugh as the boy lifted on to his toes and flung back the wet hair from his brow. He dived and his naked body was swallowed by the restless glitter.

★   ★   ★

Cynthia was on the phone to mother; had been speaking for a good 20 minutes. " ... Yes ... Yes. It really was a lovely trip ... Heavenly! It's the most lovely country. Callum? Oh he was in his glory. But you know he can be infuriating. He dragged me all the way to goodness knows where and then wouldn't tell me a thing about what he'd been doing.

"I don't know, I wouldn't go any farther than the shops. He didn't even pay any attention to the cardigan I bought. Cost him the earth, too. He came back looking as if he'd seen a ghost or something ... not a word. He can be trying, but he is such a dear really ... "

She went on for a good quarter of an hour more (it was a local call). She had plenty time. Callum was sitting happily on the underground travelling from Buchanan Street to Kinning Park, his brief case on his knee and the evening paper open at the sports page.

It had been a good day at the office.

30. Glasgow Bookshop

I don't visit Glasgow very often: yesterday's visit will sufice for the next few months, I hope. Glaswegians are marvellous people and it is one of the most human of cities. My mother's mother came from somewhere off the Great Western Road, so I'm biased; I like Glasgow.

But I am basically a Fifer and have to live where the North Sea can periodically flatten the poor garden and topple over my home-built "Cat" in the Forth. I can lie in bed and watch Inchkeith's light flicker its time pattern on the wall.

It was to give a lecture to the Langbank Sailing Club that I'd wangled a day off to go to Glasgow. After some business in the city centre I was driving out when a book and junk shop caught my eye. I've a good library of sea books and try never to pass anything by, especially old junk shops. I remember finding—no, never mind, nautical book chat is like sailors' tales. . . .

I swung off the road to find somewhere to park. A football, followed by chatter of young Pakistani kids had me stopping sharply. Curses from the car behind, curses from me—and what I took for curses in return. I pulled in where a notice said: "No Barking." (Behind it on the wall, there were chalked an assortment of obscenities).

At the bottom of the hill the new ring road was stalking on its concrete legs, kicking down old buildings and tenements, their windows smashed into dirty jig-saws, old mouldings perched or fallen in the clearances. There was a background of piping voices, of sparrows' chatter, of distant traffic. A hot and grimy Glasgow evening.

I went down past a school. A priest was kicking a ball about behind the high cage wire of the playground. A traffic warden waved me across.

"It's a braw day," he greeted.

The shop was like a derelict barge left by the tide. Rubble car parks or teeming streets of cars surrounded its old rotting structure. A solitary wedge of building, shuttered and boarded, empty— except for this vent from which goods had spilled out into the pavement in wild disorder. There were three cases of books against the wall, so stepping over a pile of crockery and an evil-smelling pram. I scanned the volumes quickly. Nothing, so I went inside.

It was not always easy to see the books for the items piled up in front of them or dangling from nails on the shelves. There were acres of books really if you could squeeze down the crowded corridors. In just such a place I'd found a "Slocum" beautifully bound in leather—and paid for the leather not the contents.

There was a back-room from which came the sound of several voices, dominated by a thick husky female's.

"Tak yer books ben." I was told by the dusty-suited man busy carting in the goods, load by load. "Whit a bloody life," he added. "Every bloody day tae cairt them bloody oot and then cairt them bloody ben."

"Aye, it's a bloody shame," I sympathised—and went ben.

Another room of books and crowded teachests, crowded cabinets, crowded drawers. There was quite an armoury too with several old muskets and spears. The room was crowded with a handful of people, dominated by a dame with extraordinary red hair, and an extraordinary deep filing voice. She was extraordinarily inebriated.

My entry was not even noticed. I was bewildered enough just to stand in this annexe to Babel.

An American woman in a grey cloth suit and rakish hat was prodding a fleshy youth in his fleshiest parts.

"What I say is that Jesus Christ was a mighty fine person. Otherwise how could his influence have lasted all these years? You can't deny that now, can ya? Is that not enough?"

"I don't think so," the youth began, to be interrupted by Madam.

"These latter-day saints are all the same; talk, talk. You canna tell him anything my dear. Noo, try some of ma guid tobaccy. Dutch. You dinna smoke a pipe? Well, b—— you then for a b—— yankee. What ah say is this. Never, ever, wid ah buy a German car like yon Volkswagen or Mercedes or Renault."

Another man came in to interrupt and correct. It was like a sandbag in the Nile.

"If its not f——ing German it should be with a name like that. Think what Hitler did to us Jews then. I'm no a practising Jew but I'm loyal to some things."

"Christ demands a bit more than just a casual nod. He was a bit more than a man just."

"Ah, shut up, you. Whit dae ye think this is? This pipe willna draw. Hae ye got a match, Eck? Stop rummaging aboot in ma drawers. Naebody gangs through ma drawers. Will ye look at thaat? He just does whit he likes. Never buys onything either ..."

"Well when were you last in my place?"

"Ah wouldna' be seen deid in Pitlochry. Ye're too pricey fur me. Rich Americans is your line. Pardon me, my dear, I ken you're yin, but it's no yir fault. Ye're yin o us. A right decent Jew is worth ..."

"But I'm not ..."

"Dinna haver! Ye're a Jew if I say you are. Ah dinna want a match. Whit's my damn lighter fur, dae ye think? Drunk? Me? But of course. Have ye ever known me else? Eck, come oot o there! He jist does whit he likes. It's as weel I ken him."

She suddenly spotted me.

"An' wha the devil are you? I've no see ye afore? Where are ye frae?"

"Fife."

"I wouldna trust a Fifer. But I like Fife fine. Fife's a braw place. It's right bonnie up by Montrose way, ah say. Whit dae ye want? Dinna gape at me. Aye, it's flat. Nae heid left." (This of her glass of beer.)

"Can I have these books?" I ventured, placing my seven chosen volumes beside her. They had prices pencilled inside. A bit too much but some I was keen on. There had been others I'd sadly said "no" to. She plonked them down at her slipper-clad feet.

"Ah havena my specs the day. An whit are you? A damn student or summit? Ye dinna sound like a Fifer."

"I've lived abroad a lot."

"Whaur? London? Look at me. I've been aw roon the world and where dae I end up? In Glesca, bloody, bloody Glesca. Let that be a lesson tae ye.

"Sold oot tae the bulldozers. Whit will happen tae aw ma books? I've twenty thoosan ye ken. I've read every yin. Never sell books. Wullie, ye big haddy, will ye watch hoo ye bash the brasses? An dinna girn at me. If I could rise I'd bloody well f———you."

"Ye'd better haud yir tongue," said a lean lad. "Ye're ower drunk tae be let loose on customers the day."

"These are no jist customers I'll hae ye ken. We were discussin deep matters, were we no hen?"

"Aye one pint deep."

"*Hen*, say that's a cute expression. Is it a Scottish phrase of endearment?"

"Are ye tryin to mak a fool o me? If so I'll no say anither word to a damn Yankee as long as I live an tae hell wi entent cordiality. Maybe I'm a bitty drunk. An why no? This is condemned property ye ken. Ma wee books. Wha's tae look after ma wee books when I'm awa? They say I've got cancer. Havers, it's aw havers, Anno domini is ma complaint. Anno domini an my daily pints. Mind today its been a bit mair but then we've got veesitors from Americy. An Fife. You're a rum Fifer you are. Can you no buy mair stuff?"

"Maybe I can't afford any more."

"Well, let's see what you've got the noo."

She picked up my books one at a time, screwed up her eyes, looked at me, sniffed, giggled and quoted what seemed random prices: "Ten bob," "five bob." These quotes bore no relation to priced marked on the book: some double in price and I just mutely shook my head.

Others I equally nodded in bewilderment at as she virtually threw them away. I suppose it balanced out, but to a collector it was agony. We ended with two piles. There was nothing wrong with her arithmetic, drunk or sober.

"Twa quid tae ye laddie. Na. Na. Dinna gie the money tae me. Ah canna bide this new money. Wullie work the till fur me like a good lad. It's a converted machine but I canna understan it at aw. A fiver, eh? A fiver frae a Fifer? Ah should hae charged ye mair. Weel, awa ben there where my best books are. Fancy stuff, ye ken."

I went through wondering what I'd find. Religion? Or rare editions? Pornography, perhaps? It was very anticlimax; just dull Victorian, dusty in every sense. Probably untouched for years and possibly only valuable for an expert. I browsed, took out a copy of a MacGregor's canoe epic in his "Rob Roy" (could risk 50p at the most for it's worth two pounds).

She was still rasping forth as I went through.

"Ah bet he's some Government snooper, Fifer my fit! Oh, hello son! Ye've found summat? Aye, it's a braw book. Twa quid tae ye."

"Two quid!" I echoed.

"Like it or lump it."

"I'll lump it, thank you."

"Nae need tae thank me. Never trust a German or a toon cooncil is whit ah say. Weel, Fifer, are ye goin tae stan aw day?"

She handed me an ill-wrapped parcel and I stomped out. The pavement was clear. The sad man who had laboriously taken everything in was standing at the door.

"She's a bloody, drunken bloody . . ." he tailed off. "She didna tak tae ye?"

"I don't think so."

"Ah weel. She doesna tak tae me an I've been merrit tae her twenty-twa bloody year. Cheeri-bye."

I went off to lecture. It took an effort to concentrate—but driving home I had a chance to recall the bookshop; chuckled at the memory.

Tonight I untied my parcel after tea, ready for a lazy evening's enjoyment. Not one book in the parcel had been picked by me. I'd never set eyes on them before.